FAHRE

NOTES

including
- *Life and Background*
- *Introduction to Bradbury's Fiction*
- *Introduction to the Novel*
- *List of Characters*
- *Critical Commentaries*
- *Critical Analyses*
- *Critical Essays*
   Dystopian Fiction and *Fahrenheit 451*
   The Issue of Censorship
- *Review Questions and Essay Topics*
- *Bradbury's Published Works*
- *Selected Bibliography*
- *Selected Bibliography on Intellectual Freedom
   and Censorship*

by
Samuel J. Umland, Ph.D.
Department of English
University of Nebraska

INCORPORATED

LINCOLN, NEBRASKA 68501

Editor

Gary Carey, M.A.
University of Colorado

Consulting Editor

James L. Roberts, Ph.D.
Department of English
University of Nebraska

CONTENTS

Centerfold: *Fahrenheit 451* Character Web

FAHRENHEIT 451

Notes

LIFE AND BACKGROUND

Ray Douglas Bradbury, one of America's finest writers, was born on August 22, 1920, in the town of Waukegan, Illinois. Often said to be this country's best science fiction writer, Bradbury has also earned acclaim in the fields of poetry, drama, and screenwriting. As a young boy, Bradbury's life revolved around magic, magicians, circuses, and other such fantasies. Whenever traveling circuses pitched their tents in Waukegan, Bradbury and his brother were always on hand. When he was eleven, and Blackstone the Magician came to town, Bradbury attended every performance. Mr. Electrico, another magician of sorts, particularly impressed Bradbury with his death-defying electric chair act. In fact, this magician once gave young Bradbury such a convincing talk that Bradbury decided to become a magician—the best in the world!

Bradbury's love of fantasy was given encouragement by his family. Their favorite time of the year was Halloween, and they celebrated it with even more enthusiasm than they celebrated Christmas. When Bradbury was eight, his Aunt Neva helped him devise the grandest Halloween party imaginable. The Bradbury home was transformed into a haunted house with grinning pumpkins, ghost-like sheets hanging in the cellar, and raw chicken meat representing parts of a dead witch. In years to come, such details as these were used to furnish material for Bradbury's stories.

In addition to Bradbury's magician heroes, Buck Rogers, Flash Gordon, and Tarzan ranked high on his list of favorites. Bradbury read the series of books about the Emerald City of Oz, and his Aunt Neva read him the terror-filled tales of Poe. All of these stories with their fantastic characters and settings were dramatic influences on Bradbury's later life.

Bradbury began his writing career in 1931 at the age of eleven, using butcher paper that had to be unrolled as his story progressed. The following year, he and his family moved from Illinois to Arizona, and that same year, Bradbury received a toy typewriter on which he wrote his first stories.

In 1934, when Bradbury was fourteen, his family moved from Arizona to Los Angeles, and here his writing career began to solidify. In 1937, he became a member of the Los Angeles Science Fiction League, whose help enabled him to publish four issues of his own science-fiction fan magazine, or "fanzine," *Futuria Fantasia*. His first professional sale was for a short story entitled "Pendulum," co-authored with Henry Hasse; it appeared in *Super Science Stories*, August, 1941, the issue appearing on Bradbury's twenty-first birthday. From then on, Bradbury's fantasy works were published in numerous magazines throughout the country.

Bradbury says that he learned to write by recalling his own experiences. It's no surprise, then, that many of his early stories are based on his childhood experiences in Illinois. For example, "The Jar" (*Weird Tales*, 1944) is based on the first time that Bradbury saw a pickled embryo, displayed in a sideshow of one of the carnivals that visited his hometown. "Homecoming" (*Mademoiselle*, 1946) was inspired by his relatives' marvelous Halloween parties, and "Uncle Einar" (*Dark Carnival*, 1947), a story about a man with green wings, is based loosely on one of Bradbury's uncles.

In 1947, after *Dark Carnival* (a collection of weird and macabre stories) was published, Bradbury turned to another kind of writing—philosophical science fiction. One work in particular, *The Martian Chronicles* (1950), grew out of Bradbury's own personal philosophy and his concern for the future of humankind.

Two other highly personal works, *Dandelion Wine* (1957) and *Something Wicked This Way Comes* (1962), also exemplify his belief that writing should come from a writer's own philosophy and from his own experiences. Both of these novels are set in fictitious Green Town—which is, in reality, Bradbury's hometown of Waukegan, Illinois. The ravine that is described in both books is located on Yeoman Creek, and the library, which is an important setting in *Something Wicked This Way Comes*, used to be located on Waukegan's Sheridan Road.

In addition to Bradbury's many books and his hundreds of short stories, works such as *The Beast from 20,000 Fathoms, It Came from Outer Space, Fahrenheit 451, The Illustrated Man,* and *Something Wicked This Way Comes* have been made into major motion pictures. In addition, Bradbury has also written for television, radio, and the theater.

Clearly, Bradbury kept his promise to Mr. Electrico. He did become a magician, using his pen as a magic wand to transport his readers into wondrous situations. Bradbury himself attests to this fact in an article appearing in the 1952 *Ray Bradbury Review.* He says that he simply transferred his "methods of magic from the stage of a sheet of Eaton's Bond paper—for there is something of the magician in every writer, flourishing his effects and making his miracles."

Today, Bradbury lives in Los Angeles, is a Sunday painter, and collects Mexican artifacts. He has four grown daughters and several grandchildren. Among Bradbury's latest works are *Death Is a Lonely Business* (1985), *The April Witch* (1987), *Death Has Lost Its Charm* (1987), *The Toynbee Convector* (1988), *Graveyard for Lunatics* (1990), *Folon's Folons* (1990), *Zen in the Art of Writing: Essays on Creativity* (1991), and *A Chrestomathy of Ray Bradbury: A Dramatic Selection* (1991).

INTRODUCTION TO BRADBURY'S FICTION

It has become commonplace to call Ray Bradbury a "science fiction author," which is an inaccurate label; to pigeonhole his writings as "science fiction" is to obscure rather than clarify Bradbury's work. It might be useful to take a brief overview of Bradbury's fiction in order to sort out the various types of fiction he writes and consider various ways of understanding his work—rather than lumping it fallaciously into the narrow category of science fiction.

The perceptive critic Peter Nicholls, writing in the *Science Fiction Encyclopedia* (Doubleday, 1979), is reluctant to place Bradbury's work in the science fiction genre; on the contrary, he finds Bradbury's themes to be "traditionally American" and says that Bradbury's choosing "to render them [his themes] on several important occasions in sf [science fiction] imagery does not make RB [Bradbury] a sf writer, even though his early years were devoted to the form." Nicholls concludes that Bradbury is, in fact, a "whimsical fantasist in an older tradition."

Humanist Gilbert Highet, in his "Introduction" to *The Vintage Bradbury* (Vintage, 1965), agrees with Nicholls. He finds Bradbury to have such illustrious European predecessors as Villiers de l'Isle-Adam (1840–89), E.T.A. Hoffman (1776–1822), H. G. Wells (1866–1946), and (Joseph) Rudyard Kipling (1865–1936); early American fantasists include Edgar Allan Poe (1809–49), Ambrose Bierce (1842–1914), H. P. Lovecraft (1890–1937), and Charles G. Finney (1905–). The latter's *Circus of Dr. Lao* (1935) was a major influence on Bradbury's works. One might note, too, that the only science fiction writers whom Bradbury consistently mentions are those whom he considers his "teachers"—Leigh Brackett and Henry Kuttner.

The literary critic and writer J. B. Priestley has observed that despite the fact that Bradbury is often identified as a science fiction writer, Bradbury "is concerned not with gadgets but with men's feelings. He creates imaginatively, and it may be assumed that he is not merely turning out stuff for a new and flourishing [science fiction] market but is trying to express some of his own deepest feelings." Priestly goes on to suggest that behind all of Bradbury's tales are "deep feelings of anxiety, fear, and guilt."

Bradbury's characters are earnest in their quest for a way in which they can effectively deal with the problem of evil. They are hungry to know who they are and how they can achieve their full potential, and yet, simultaneously, these same brave human beings are terribly afraid of growing old and dying.

As a result of the themes with which Bradbury consistently deals, his works often take on a strongly evangelical tone, for he always insists that the only hope for the world lies within the individual. "I realize very late in life now that I could have made a fine priest or minister," confesses Bradbury. The truth of this claim lies in Bradbury's exposing humanity for what it is while offering moral encouragement by showing us what we *can* be. That is, Bradbury attempts to present humankind with a vision of the best possible of all worlds, a utopia—and, for Bradbury, this utopia is attainable. Furthermore, Bradbury's philosophical idealism insists that once we have discovered and attained this utopia within ourselves, our universe will accordingly improve. However, before we can achieve Bradbury's utopia, we must first conquer, or at least learn to cope adequately, with the evil that confronts us at every hour with feelings of loneliness and unfulfillment. This "evil" is usually the inability to know ourselves fully, the fear of growing old, and the fear of death.

The focus on death is threaded throughout Bradbury's writings and alongside it is Bradbury's deep interest in the themes of deceit, dissatisfaction with the self, the reality of evil and how to contend with it, and the attainment of self-knowledge. As one might expect, these concepts are embodied in traditional images: ravine imagery, mirror imagery, water imagery, carnival imagery, sun and fire imagery, and the opposition of light and dark, good and evil.

In particular, both the physical and psychological aspects of death and dying are examined through Bradbury's use of ravine imagery. Bradbury believes that if we can face and understand our own individual, ultimate deaths, then we can appreciate ourselves and our lives to a fuller degree. He believes that it is necessary to "meet and know and chew and swallow death as a writer and as a reader" and to exorcise it from the subconscious so that we will not have to think about it all the time. Only then can we continue with our real business—which is, living.

Frequently, Bradbury also uses imagery associated with masks. Masks, of course, are often associated with deceit, deception, and games. To put on a mask is to be able to mimic, but if we put on a mask, we permit ourselves to disguise our feelings and, therefore, in Bradbury's works, a mask is always an attractive but a dangerous element.

Mirror imagery in Bradbury's stories frequently illustrates the theme of dissatisfaction with ourselves. In some instances, too, Bradbury employs mirror imagery as an emblem of reality, depicting our fascination with what mirrors tell us about ourselves. However, mention of this mirror imagery is not complete without also mentioning the antithesis of reality—that is, fantasy. Bradbury's mirror also allows us to envision ourselves in all the splendor that we wish to see ourselves and how we wish to be seen by others. And inherent in any analysis of mirror imagery is Bradbury's conservative view that we are only who we are, and any attempt at altering ourselves can lead only to disaster.

Bradbury's carnival imagery is a vivid device that he often uses in order to effectively focus on the presence of evil as a real force in the world. A study of his carnival imagery reveals his belief that the potential for evil exists in a dormant form in each of us; he believes that unless we keep that which is good within us in fit condition by actively exercising it, we will lose our ability to combat evil, thus allowing evil to grow and become powerful.

The battle between good and evil appears in several images contained in Bradbury's works. One such image is the sun, which functions symbolically as a source of life and also as a symbol for the wholeness of humankind. Very simply, for Bradbury, light is good and dark is evil.

A number of Bradbury's stories go a step further, using sun imagery as a symbol for God and the promise of immortality. Similarly, Bradbury's fire imagery focuses on the theme of the victory of good over evil. Appropriately, Bradbury's fire imagery and his sun imagery function hand-in-hand since fire can symbolically be considered as the sun's earthly representative. The works which deal most specifically with fire imagery contain Bradbury's most important social commentaries concerning the condition of the world as he sees it. His most intense pleas in favor of the arts and humanities, as opposed to sterile technology, occur in stories which use sun and fire imagery.

Another image that Bradbury often uses to show the possibilities for overcoming evil in the world is the image of the smile. Smiles and laughter, according to Bradbury, derive their power from their progenitor—love. Bradbury believes that love is the strongest and most humanizing force which man possesses.

Our knowledge of death as a part of life, our learning to make the best of who and what we are, our acceptance of evil as well as good in the world, and our battle to arrest evil are the discoveries which give us a broader insight into ourselves.

This self-knowledge is also presented in Bradbury's stories through the use of water imagery. Water imagery is used by Bradbury in the traditional sense—that is, to suggest the life source itself and the transition of the life cycle from one phase to another. Water imagery also depicts the theme of rebirth, regeneration, and purification and is also used throughout Bradbury's writings. This image is incorporated into his "celebrate life" theme. Bradbury urges us to enjoy being alive in spite of life's difficulties—rather than finding life a drudgery because of its difficulties.

Bradbury has high hopes for the future of man and for man's acquisition of the most fulfilling life possible—a utopia. He shows his reader a utopian world that can result if we heed his advice, and he describes the horrors that could ensue if certain contemporary tendencies are not stopped. Bradbury always suggests that Earth could be the best of all possible worlds, and he also suggests that humankind, when it has come to grips with itself, can make the world a place in which we can all be as free and as happy as we have ever dreamed of becoming.

INTRODUCTION TO THE NOVEL

Critics find Bradbury's most interesting years the post-World War II years, 1947–57, a period which roughly corresponds to a time when science fiction authors were beginning to approach their subject matter seriously and were creating characters who had psychological complexity and ambiguity. During this decade, Bradbury produced some of his most vital works: *Dark Carnival* (Arkham House, 1947); the amazing *Martian Chronicles* (Doubleday, 1950), his first and perhaps his finest science fiction work; the short story collections *The Illustrated Man* (Doubleday, 1951), *The Golden Apples of the Sun* (Doubleday, 1953), and *Dandelion Wine* (Doubleday, 1957), a short novel that has attained the status of being a minor American classic.

It was during this period that Bradbury also produced "The Fireman," a short story that appeared in *Galaxy Science Fiction's* second issue in February 1951 and was expanded into *Fahrenheit 451* (October 1953), his best and best-known novel. Initially published by Ballentine with two other stories, "The Playground" and "And the Rock Cried Out," *Fahrenheit 451* was not published separately until the Ballantine paperback release in April 1960.

Interestingly, the impetus for the characters and the situation of *Fahrenheit 451* date earlier than "The Fireman." They first appeared during the years immediately following World War II, as Bradbury reveals in his introduction to *Pillar of Fire and Other Plays* (Bantam, 1975):

> This story ["Pillar of Fire," *Planet Stories*, Summer 1948], this character . . . I see now were rehearsals for my later novel and film *Fahrenheit 451*. If Montag is a burner of books who wakens to reading and becomes obsessed with saving mind-as-printed-upon-matter,

> then Lantry [protagonist of "Pillar of Fire"] is the books themselves, he is the thing to be saved. In an ideal world, he and Montag would have met, set up shop and lived happily ever after: library and saver of libraries, book and reader, idea and flesh to preserve the idea.

By Bradbury's own admission, the thematic obsession which explicitly emerges in *Fahrenheit 451* is the burning of books, the destruction of "mind-as-printed-upon-matter," to use Bradbury's accurate, vivid phrasing. And although Bradbury never uses the word "censorship" in the novel, one should be aware that he is deeply concerned with censorship. "Book burning" is, of course, a hyperbolic phrase which describes the suppression of writing. The real issue of the novel is censorship.

If one reads "Pillar of Fire" sensitively, it is not all books that are in danger in the future "dystopia," but particular kinds, or genres, of books. This, of course, is not precisely true of *Fahrenheit 451;* here, it is *all* books that are burned by the "firemen." This novel might be understood as a kind of hyperbolic extension of the tensions of the earlier story.

The above observation about "Pillar of Fire" (1948) needs to be explored at some length, for one must ask what are the social and/or economic forces which caused such a thematic obsession to emerge in Bradbury's work from the period 1948–53? Why is it only books of imagination, of fantasy, of the macabre and occult, which are threatened in "Pillar of Fire"?

It should be noted that works by fantasists are also threatened in Bradbury's story "Usher II" (1950), which appears in *The Martian Chronicles* (also 1950). "Pillar of Fire" thus becomes a rehearsal for the themes of "Usher II," and the latter story appears to inhabit the same imaginative realm as does "The Fireman" of 1951, although "The Fireman" was obviously written during the same period as "Usher II," 1950, and is, in fact, copyrighted 1950. Indeed, the character of William Lantry in "Pillar of Fire" and the character of William Stendahl in "Usher II" are quite similar, as are the authors whose books are threatened—Poe, Bierce, and other American fantasists. Moreover, a "Burning Crew" is referred to in "Usher II," one which will come to burn Stendahl's beloved library of imaginative literature. The "Burning Crew" is obviously a synonym for the "firemen" of *Fahrenheit 451.*

The question might be asked in another way: "Why is Bradbury sensitive to the popular condemnation of fantasy literature?" By extension, of course, this becomes an issue of the literary "merit" of works of popular literature. Why is Bradbury particularly sensitive to the critical reception of fantasy literature during the post–World War II period? The question becomes even more problematic when one considers that Bradbury himself was publishing science fiction and fantasy in "legitimate" magazines, or "slicks," such as *Colliers* and *The Saturday Evening Post*, not in the "pulps." As Peter Nicholls observes: "[Bradbury's] career remains the biggest breakthrough into lush markets made by any genre sf writer" (1985).

We have, of course, come far astray from a formal discussion of *Fahrenheit 451*, but the questions are not unrelated and perhaps offer another way of reading the novel than the traditional one: as genre science fiction. After all, Bradbury's obsessions with the suppression of fantasy literature may express, at the psychological level, the wrestling with the validity of his own career as a fantasist. We need hardly remind the reader that *Fahrenheit 451* represents Bradbury's first published novel (indeed, one of his few novels), written at a time when—according to Brian W. Aldiss (Schocken, 1974)—"science fiction was still a minority cult, little known to any but its devotees." And, in the brief authorial statement which is appended to the beginning of *The October Country* (Ballantine, 1955), an abridgement of his earlier collection *Dark Carnival* (1947), Bradbury feels compelled to tell his readers that *The October Country* will present a side of my writing that is probably unfamiliar to them, and a type of story that I rarely have done since 1948." It is clear that by 1955 (during a time when his earliest work was out-of-print), Bradbury was aware of his (perhaps undeserved) reputation as a science fiction writer and was attempting to present to his readership an aspect of his work with which they would have been unfamiliar. It is no wonder that his next published book after *The October Country*, *Dandelion Wine* (Doubleday, 1957) is *not* science fiction, but a tour de force of juvenalia—specifically, a celebration of adolescence and the life-affirming value of the imagination. With the exception of *A Medicine for Melancholy* (Doubleday, 1959), a collection of short stories dominated by science fiction selections, Bradbury has rarely returned to science fiction. (Collections such as *R is for Rocket* [1962] and *S is for Space* [1966] only recycle earlier stories.)

But there may be another aspect of this novel which is equally as interesting: that the suppression and condemnation of imaginative literature—viewed earlier as a synecdoche for popular literature—represent the development of an increasingly oppressive political organization which wishes to deny originality and idiosyncrasy. *Fahrenheit 451* uses the science fiction motif of "dystopia"—a totalitarian, highly centralized and therefore oppressive social organization which sacrifices individual expression for the sake of efficiency and social "harmony," all of which is achieved through technocratic means. The reader might examine those episodes of *Dandelion Wine*—the book most contiguous with *Fahrenheit 451* (disregarding *The October Country*)—originally published as "The Happiness Machine" and "The Trolley." The former story views technology as unable to provide for—and is even opposed to—human happiness; the latter story views technological innovation, for the sake of "efficiency," as oppressive, perhaps even proto-fascist. In fact, one might view *Dandelion Wine*, published after Bradbury became labeled as a formidable science fiction writer, as viewing technology and technological innovation as inconsequential, even unimportant, in solving basic human problems. (For example, note in *Fahrenheit 451* the marital problems between Montag and his wife—even though their home is full of technological contrivances specifically designed for domestic bliss—or explore the motivation for the development of the "Mechanical Hound" as a vehicle of social control *via* terroristic means.)

Yet, for all of these rich possibilities of exploration in this novel, the issue of "book burning," or censorship, remains most central to the novel and is the most difficult issue with which to grapple. At the risk of making a broad generalization, book burning is synonymous with irrationality in the twentieth century. The genesis of *Fahrenheit 451* must have been contiguous with the period of Nazi anti-intellectualism during the late 1930s, and book burning certainly became a synonym for anti-intellectualism in 1950s science fiction—as it was in Walter M. Miller's *A Canticle for Leibowitz* (Lippincott, 1959). It should be realized that *Fahrenheit 451* emerges during a period of extreme interest in what Brian W. Aldiss calls "an authoritarian society," roughly corresponding to the years 1945-1953, as revealed in works by George Orwell—*Animal Farm* (1945) and *1984* (1948); B. F. Skinner's *Walden Two* (1948); Kurt Vonnegut's

Player Piano (1952); Evelyn Waugh's *Love Among the Ruins* (1953); and Frederick Pohl and C. M. Kornbluth's *The Space Merchants* (1953). Moreover, the post-war period also produced several novels and films concerned with the possibilities of nuclear holocaust, which hovers over Montag's world throughout the novel.

The novel also appears during the era which historians label "the McCarthy period," the post-war political climate characterized by xenophobia, blacklisting, and censorship. In June 1949, for example, Representative John S. Wood asked some seventy colleges to submit their textbooks for examination and approval by the Un-American Activities Committee. Bradbury himself (*Nation*, May 2, 1953), in an article on science fiction as social criticism, suggested that "when the wind is right, a faint odor of kerosene is exhaled from Senator McCarthy." I suggest that many of the issues explored in the novel cannot be separated from the historical period in which it appeared. This is not to say, however, that they are no longer relevant, or timely, issues. Indeed, the novel evidently held a particular fascination for readers in the 1980s. While the novel initially went through six printings in its first twelve years (1953–1965), it went through twenty printings in the next *five* years (1966–1971) and has been in print since its initial publication.

I stated earlier that *Fahrenheit 451* is Bradbury's best-known novel—which also, incidentally, happens to be science fiction. The novel need not, nor should it be, read only by those exclusively interested in science fiction or fantasy. It is, among other things, a genuine cultural document of the early 1950s, and it is a book of great imagination regardless of its genre—or perhaps even in spite of its genre.

LIST OF CHARACTERS

Guy Montag

The protagonist, a complacent man thirty years old. He has been a fireman for ten years.

Mildred Montag ("Millie")

Guy's self-destructive wife, also thirty years old, who reveals to Montag the alienated existence of citizens in his society.

Clarisse McClellan

Montag's new neighbor, sixteen years old, a month away from seventeen, whose recalcitrance and nonconformity allow Montag to discover how jaded his view of life has become.

Captain Beatty

Montag's superior, the Fire Captain, who functions as the apologist for the dystopian culture in which Montag lives.

Unidentified Woman

A woman from "the ancient part of the city," whose martyrdom reveals to Montag the power of civil disobedience and the power of books and ideas.

Faber

An elderly man, a retired English professor who has become an underground, though ineffectual, scholar.

Granger

An ex-writer who is the unacknowledged leader of the social outcasts and "criminals."

Stoneman & Black

Montag's fellow firemen; conformists and conservatives. Together with Beatty, they form Montag's familiar working colleagues.

Mrs. Phelps & Mrs. Bowles

Friends of Millie who do not question the social structure; their husbands are called away to war.

CRITICAL COMMENTARIES

Fahrenheit 451 is currently the most famous work of social criticism that Bradbury has written. It deals with the extremely serious problem of the banning of books and the suppression of the mind—that is, with **censorship**. The novel examines a few pivotal days of a man's life, a man who is a burner of books, and therefore an instrument of suppression. In a few short days, this man is transformed from a narrow-minded and prejudiced conformist into a dynamic individual, committed to social change, to a life of saving books rather than destroying them.

You should note two things before you begin the novel: 1) the significance of the title *Fahrenheit 451*, "the temperature at which book-paper catches fire, and burns . . . " and 2) the epigram by Juan Ramón Jiménez: "If they give you ruled paper, write the other way." Jiménez (1881–1958), was a Spanish poet; he won the Nobel Prize for Literature in 1956 and was largely responsible for introducing Modernism into Spanish poetry. The implications of both of these concepts—one, a simple fact; the other, a challenge to authority—gain immense significance by the conclusion of the book.

PART I: THE HEARTH AND THE SALAMANDER

The point of view of this short novel is that of Guy Montag, a thirty-year-old "fireman" in the twenty-fourth century (remember that the novel was written in the early 1950s). In this futuristic dystopic (miserable, oppressive) setting, homes have been fireproofed with a thin plastic sheath so that there is no longer the demand for a fireman to do his former work—putting *out* fires. Instead, firemen *start* fires: they have been given a new task; they are the caretakers of this future society's peace of mind. They burn books as a means of maintaining social order; they are the official censors of the state. Guy Montag's job as a fireman is to seek out and destroy any home in which books have been found. Books are evil; they must be destroyed.

For the pyromaniac Montag, "It was a pleasure to burn." For Montag and others like him, the burning of books is good. Without books, and therefore without ideas, everyone conforms; as a consequence, everyone is happy. When books and ideas are available to people, conflict and unhappiness occur. In theory, then, Montag, in all his destructive fury, should be happy, and so it would seem: when he views himself in the firehouse mirror after a night of burning, he grins "the fierce grin of all men singed and driven back by flame," and thinks that all firemen, everywhere, must look like white men masquerading as minstrels, grinning behind their "burnt-corked" masks.

Later, as Montag goes to sleep, he realizes that his smile is still gripping his face muscles, even in the dark. The language here—"fiery smile still gripped by his face muscles"—suggests that his smile is artificial and forced. Soon he will understand that this small bit of truth is an immense truth for himself. At present, Montag *seems* to enjoy his job as a fireman. He is a "smiling fireman." However, the discomfort of the smile and, later, the realization of its artificiality foreshadow Montag's eventual dissatisfaction not only with his job but also with his life. Montag smiles, but he is not happy. The smile, just like his "burnt-corked" face, is a mask.

We discover almost immediately—when Montag meets the teenage girl, Clarisse McClellan, who is his new neighbor—that he is not happy. Clarisse is portrayed as spontaneous and naturally curious; Montag as insincere and jaded. Clarisse has no rigid daily schedule; Montag (so it would seem) is a creature of habit. She speaks to him of the beauties of life, the man in the moon, the early morning dew, and her liking to smell things and look at things. Montag has never concerned himself with such "insignificant" matters.

Clarisse lives with her mother, father, and uncle; Montag has no family other than his wife, and, as we shall soon discover, his home life is unhappy. Clarisse accepts Montag for what he is; Montag finds Clarisse's peculiarities (that is, her individuality) slightly annoying: "You think too many things," he tells her.

Yet, for all of these differences, the two are attracted to one another. Her vivacity is infectious, and Montag finds her unusual perspectives about life intriguing. Indeed, she will be partly responsible for Montag's change in attitude. She arouses Montag's curiosity and begins to help him discover that real happiness has been missing from his life for quite some time. Moreover, it seems that, for Montag, there is something in Clarisse that is a long-repressed part of himself: "How like a mirror, too, her face. Impossible; for how many people did you know who refracted your own light to you?"

At the very least, Clarisse awakens in Montag a love and a desire to enjoy the very simple, very innocent things in life. She speaks to him about her delight in just letting the rain fall upon her face and into her mouth. Later, Montag, too, turns his head upward into the early November rain in order to catch a mouthful of the cool liquid. In effect, Clarisse, in just a very few meetings, exerts a powerful influence on Montag, and he is never able to find happiness in his former life again.

Yet if the water imagery of this early scene implies rebirth or regeneration, it is also associated with the artificiality of the peoples' lives in this future dystopia. The reader discovers that each night before she goes to bed, Mildred Montag ("Millie") places small, seashell-like radios into her ears, and the music whisks her away from the dreariness of her everyday reality. As Montag lies in bed, the room seems empty because the waves of sound "came in and bore her [Mildred] off on their great tides of sound, floating her, wide-eyed, toward morning." Mildred has not let one night pass in the last two years in which she has failed to swim "that sea, [and has] not gladly gone down in it for the third time." However, the music that Mildred feels to be life-giving actually robs her of the knowledge and meaning of life. She has abandoned reality through the use of these tiny, technological wonders which instill mindlessness.

Although she would never—or could never—admit it, Millie Montag is not happy either. Her need for the seashell radios in order to sleep is insignificant when measured against her addiction to tranquilizers and sleeping pills. On this night, in particular, Montag discovers that she has taken an overdose of tranquilizers and calls the emergency ward. Millie is saved by two impersonal technicians who bring machines to pump her stomach and to provide a total transfusion, but it is quite possible she could overdose again—and never even know it. Or so it would seem. The matter of the overdose—whether it is an attempted suicide or a result of sheer mindlessness—is never settled. Though Montag wishes to discuss the matter of the overdose, Millie does not, and their inability to agree on even this matter suggests the profound estrangement that exists between them.

Montag comes to realize this. He discovers that their marriage is a shambles: he cannot even remember when or where (or how) he and Millie met. Millie cannot remember it either. She is more interested in her "family"—the illusory images on her three-wall TV. This three-wall TV is another means that Mildred uses to escape reality (and perhaps her unhappiness with life and with Montag). She neglects, or perhaps avoids, Montag and, instead, lavishes her attention upon her television "relatives." The television family which never says anything or does anything significant, the high-speed abandon with which she drives their car, and even the overdose of sleeping pills she takes—all of these become indicators for Montag that their life is both meaningless and purposeless. They do not love each other; they probably don't love anything, except perhaps burning (Montag) and living second-hand (Millie).

Yet, for Montag, these discoveries are difficult to express; he is only dimly cognizant of his unhappiness—and Millie's—when he has the first incident with the "Mechanical Hound." The Mechanical Hound is best understood as a device of terror, a machine whose perverse similarity to a trained killer-dog is improved by a refined technology that allows it to inexorably track down and capture criminals by stunning them with a tranquilizer. In some sense, the Hound's distrust of Montag—its "growl"—is a barometer of Montag's growing unhappiness. Montag also believes that somehow the Hound knows that he has confiscated some books during one of his raids.

Captain Beatty, the Fire Chief, intuitively senses Montag's growing discontent with his life and job. Beatty, who functions as the apologist of the future dystopia, is an intelligent, but ultimately cynical man. He is, paradoxically, well-read and is even willing to allow Montag to have some slight curiosity about what is in books. Yet, for Beatty, as a defender of the state, one who has compromised his morality for social stability, all intellectual curiosity, all hunger for knowledge, must be quelled for the good of the state, for conformity. He even allows for the perversion of history, as it appears in *Firemen of America*: "Established, 1790, to burn English-influenced books in the Colonies. First Fireman: Benjamin Franklin.." Curiosity about books can be tolerated only insofar as it doesn't affect one's actions. When it begins to affect an individual's conduct and a person's ability to conform—as it does Montag's—then that curiosity must be severely punished.

If the Hound is a barometer of Montag's growing dis-ease (Bradbury's word), then the news of Clarisse's death, coupled with the fire call to an old (unidentified) woman's house "in the ancient part of the city" brings about his conversion. This old woman is clearly a martyr, and her martyrdom profoundly affects Montag. Her cache of books has been discovered by her neighbor; now they must be burned. The woman stubbornly refuses to leave her home, choosing instead to be burned with her books. First, however, she makes a strange yet significant statement: "Play the man, Master Ridley; we shall this day light such a candle, by God's grace, in England, as I trust shall never be put out." Nicholas Ridley, the Bishop of London in the sixteenth century, was an early martyr for the Protestant faith. He was convicted of heresy and sentenced to be burned at the stake with a fellow heretic, Hugh Latimer. Latimer's words to Ridley are those alluded to by the unidentified woman here. (Note that a couple of visual metaphors for "Knowledge" have traditionally been of a woman, sometimes bathed in bright light or holding a burning torch. Ironically, the woman's words are prophetic, for through her own death by fire, Montag's discontent drives him to an investigation of what books really are, what they contain, and what fulfillment they offer.

Montag is unable to understand the change taking place within himself. With a sickening awareness, it occurs to him that "Always at night the alarm comes. Never by day! Is it because fire is prettier by night? More spectacle, a better show?" He questions why this particular fire call has been such a difficult one to make, and he wonders why his hands have seemed like separate entities, hiding one of the woman's books under his coat. Her stubborn dignity compels him to discover for himself what is in books.

If Clarisse renews his interest in the sheer excitement of life, if Mildred reveals to him the unhappiness of existence of individuals in his society, then the martyred woman represents for Montag the power of ideas, and hence, the power of books which his society struggles to suppress.

When Mildred tells Montag that the McClellans have moved away because Clarisse died in an automobile accident—she was "run over by a car"—Montag's dissatisfaction with his wife, his marriage, his job, and his life intensifies. As he becomes more aware of his unhappiness, he feels even more forced to smile the fraudulent, tight-mouthed smile that he has been wearing. He also realizes that his smile is beginning to fade.

Montag fails in his attempt to talk with Millie about the disadvantages of his fireman's job and when he tries to talk to her about the intrinsic values that one can obtain from books, Millie is incapable of understanding what Montag means. All she knows is that books are unlawful and that anyone who breaks the law must be punished. Her fear for her own safety forces her to declare that she is innocent of any wrongdoing, and she says that Montag must leave her alone.

When Montag first entertains the idea of quitting his job for awhile because Millie offers him no sympathetic understanding, he feigns illness and goes to bed. (In all fairness, however, one reason for Montag's illness is that he is nauseated by the fact that he burned the woman alive the night before. His sickness is, so to speak, his conscience weighing upon him.)

Captain Beatty, as noted earlier, has been suspicious of Montag's recent behavior and has not been unaware of the intellectual and moral changes going on in Montag; he has already recognized Montag's discontent, and thus he makes a sick call to Montag's suburban home. Beatty gives Montag a "pep talk," explaining to him that every fireman sooner or later goes through a period of intellectual curiosity and steals a book. (Beatty seems to know, miraculously, that Montag has stolen a book—or books.) Beatty emphatically stresses that books contain nothing believable. He attempts to convince Montag that they are merely stories—fictions, lies—about non-existent people. Books are figments of the imagination. He tells Montag that because everyone is angered by at least some kinds of literature, the simplest solution is to get rid of all the books—"Fire is bright and fire is clean." Ridding the world of controversy puts an end to dispute and allows people to "stay happy all the time." Fire is good. It eliminates conflict from society. Beatty even supports a sort of perverse democratic ideal: ridding the world of all controversial books and ideas makes all men equal; each man is the image of all other men. He concludes his lecture by assuring Montag that the book-burning profession is an honorable one. Montag later concludes that Beatty is, in fact, afraid of books and masks his fear with contempt. At any rate, Beatty expects Montag back to work that very evening. In effect, his visit is a warning to Montag *not* to allow himself to be seduced by books.

As a side note, notice the details of Beatty's argument: "Funerals are unhappy and pagan? Eliminate them, too. Five minutes after a person is dead he's on his way to the Big Flue, the incinerators serviced by helicopters all over the country. Ten minutes after death a man's a speck of black dust. Let's not quibble over individuals with memoriums. Forget them." Those interested in mythopoetic examinations of Bradbury's work might track down a copy of his short story "Pillar of Fire" and compare the themes of that story to the passage included here.

After Beatty leaves, Montag confesses to Mildred that he cannot explain why, but that he has stolen not one, but a small library of books for himself during the past year (the total is near twenty books, one of which is a Bible). He then begins to reveal his library, which he has hidden in the air-conditioning system. When Millie sees Montag's cache of books, she panics. Montag tries to convince her that their lives are already in such a state of disrepair that an investigation of the books could possibly be beneficial. Millie is unconvinced. What neither one of them knows is that the Mechanical Hound is ready and alert for them (probably having been sent by Captain Beatty), already on Montag's trail, seemingly knowing Montag's mind better than Montag does himself.

The major developments of Part One, then, surround the degenerated future in which books and independent thinking are forbidden. Notice, however, Bradbury's implicit hope and faith in the common man, by representing the life of a working-class fireman. Though Montag is not a man of profound thought or speech, his transformation has occurred through his innate sense of morality and growing awareness of human dignity.

Note, as well, the dual image of fire in both its destructive and purifying functions. While fire is destructive, it also warms; hence, the source of the title of Part One, "The Hearth and the Salamander." Hearth suggests home and the comforting aspect of fire, its ability to warm and cook. In ancient mythology, there was the belief that the salamander was a creature that could survive in fire. Possibly Montag himself is being described through the mention of the salamander. His job has dictated that he live in an environment of fire and destruction, but Montag now realizes that the salamander is able to remove itself from fire—and survive.

(Here and in the following chapters, difficult allusions, words, and phrases are explained, as are these below.)

- **this great python** the fire hose, which resembles a great serpent, a key image in the novel which serves as a reminder of Adam and Eve's temptation to disobey God in the Garden of Eden.

- **451 degrees Fahrenheit** the temperature at which book paper catches fire and burns.

- **pigeon-winged books** the books come alive and flap their "wings" as they are thrown into the fire. This connection between books and birds continues throughout the text, symbolizing enlightenment through reading.

- **black beetle-colored helmet** the beetle, with its prominent black horns, is connected in literature with Satan. Vehicles, too, in this dystopian society resemble beetles.

- **salamander** in an animistic concept of nature, the salamander is a visual representation of fire. In mythology, it endures the flames without burning.

- **Phoenix** a mythical multicolored bird of Arabia with a long history of artistic and literary symbolism, the Phoenix is one of a kind. At the end of its five-hundred-year existence, it perches on its nest of spices and sings until sunlight ignites the mass. After the body is consumed in flames, a worm emerges from the ashes and develops into the next Phoenix.

- **Clarisse** the girl's name derives from the Latin for "brightest."

- **Guy Montag** his name suggests two significant possibilities—Guy Fawkes, the instigator of a plot to blow up the English Houses of Parliament in 1605, and Montag, a trademark of Mead, an American paper company, which makes stationery, and also of a company that makes furnaces.

- **man in the moon** the perception of children that the contours of the moon's surface are a face, which peers down at them. The image reflects the oppressive nature of a society that burns books.

- **moonstones** opal, or feldspar with a pearly luster. The moonstone is connected with Mercury, the mythological guide who leads souls to the underworld.

- **black cobra** the "suction snake" that pumps Mildred's stomach repeats the earlier image of the python; the impersonal "handymen" who operate it have "eyes of puff adders." The fact that it has an eye suggests a sinister and invasive fiber optic tube that examines the inside of the body's organs and even the soul.

- **electronic bees** futuristic "seashell ear-thimbles" which block out thoughts and supplant them with mindless entertainment.

- **TV parlor** a multi-dimensional media family which draws the viewer into the action, thereby supplanting the viewer's real family.

- **That's what the lady said** snappy stage comeback which Mildred uses in place of normal conversation.

- **proboscis**   snout, or nose.

- **morphine or procaine**   a sedative and an anesthetic.

- **Beatty**   the fire captain, who "baits" Montag, is well named.

- **November 4th**   the firemen play cards early on Mischief Day, the eve of Guy Fawkes Day, when bonfires and burning of "guys" in effigy commemorate his Gunpowder Plot, an abortive attempt to destroy James I and his Protestant supporters, who suppressed Catholics.

- **Stoneman and Black**   the firemen's names suggest the hardness of their hearts and the color of their skin and hair from contact with smoke.

- **Benjamin Franklin**   founder of America's first fire company in Boston in 1736.

- **Play the man, Master Ridley; we shall this day light such a candle, by God's grace, in England, as I trust shall never be put out!**   Bishops Hugh Latimer and Nicholas Ridley, Protestant supporters of the late Queen Jane Grey, were burned at the stake for heresy at Oxford on October 16, 1555. They refused to endorse Queen Mary, a Catholic, claiming that she was an illegitimate daughter of Henry VIII, born after he married his late brother's wife, Catherine of Aragon. Later, Captain Beatty recites the latter portion of the quotation and indicates that he knows something of history.

- **cricket**   English slang for fair play.

- **Time has fallen asleep in the afternoon sunshine**   from Chapter 1 of *Dreamthorp*, a collection of essays by Alexander Smith, a Glasgow lacemaker.

- **Tower of Babel**   in Genesis 11:1-9, the mythic explanation of how Noah's children came to speak different languages. The word "babble" derives from Babel.

- **centrifuge**   the vision of being spun in a great gyro delineates Montag's impression of separation from reality.

- **cacophony**   mindless noise.

- **pratfall**   a sight gag from vaudeville, a form of low comedy, in which the clown humiliates himself by falling clumsily on his butt.

- **automatic reflex**   Beatty is describing how people stopped using their brains and began depending on nerve functions that require no thought.

- **theremin**   a soundproofing instrument, named for Russian inventor Leon Theremin, activated by moving the hand between two electric terminals.

- **our fingers in the dike**   an allusion to the legend about the Dutch boy who performed a noble, selfless public service in holding back the sea by keeping his finger in a hole in the dike.

- **It is computed, that eleven thousand persons have at several times suffered death rather than submit to break their eggs at the smaller end**   Jonathan Swift illustrates the pettiness of human controversy in Book I, Chapter 4 of *Gulliver's Travels*. The satire found in Swift's writing emphasizes the absurd extent to which society will go to enforce conformity.

PART II: THE SIEVE AND THE SAND

Millie and Montag spend the rest of that cold, rainy November afternoon reading through the books that Montag acquired. As Montag reads, he begins to understand what Clarisse meant when she said that she knew the way life is to be experienced. (The influence of Clarisse McClellan on Montag is obviously profound.) So entranced are they by the substance of the books, they ignore "a faint scratching" outside the front door and "a slow, probing sniff, an exhalation of electric steam" under the doorsill. Millie's reaction is: "It's only a dog." Only a dog? It's the Mechanical Hound outside, probably programmed by Beatty to collect evidence that he can use later against Montag.

The Montags, however, cannot ignore the sounds of bombers crossing the sky over their house, signaling the imminence of war. The country is filled with unrest, a parallel to the growing unrest and anger smoldering within Montag.

Abandonment of reality has become uppermost in Millie's mind. When Montag speaks to her about the value and merit in books, she begins to shriek, condemning him for possessing the books, and Bradbury describes her as "sitting there like a wax doll melting in its own heat." Here, fire imagery again implies destruction. This time, though, Millie herself carries the seeds of her own destruction within her. She *could* choose books—and life—but she has selected, instead, to close her mind to the truths contained in books, placing her loyalties with the "White Clown" and the rest of her television "family." Consequently, she is described as a doll that melts in heat that it and it alone has generated. Such, however, is not the case with Montag. He now wants to understand more fully what the books are telling him; more importantly, if he is to do this, he realizes that he needs a teacher. But where can he turn?

At this point in his desperation, in his thirst for knowledge, Montag recalls an encounter with an elderly man in the park last year. The old man said that he was a retired English professor named Faber, who "had been thrown out upon the world forty years ago when the last liberal arts college shut for lack of students and patronage." Montag recalls Faber's "cadenced voice" and "convictions"; in particular, Faber's words seemed a great deal like poetry. He had said to Montag, "I don't talk *things*, sir; I talk the *meaning* of things. I sit here and *know* I'm alive." Montag remembers that he has Faber's phone number in his files of possible book hoarders, and he determines that if anyone can be his teacher, Faber can. Consequently, Montag takes the subway to Faber's home, carrying a copy of the Bible with him.

While riding the subway to Faber's house, Montag has a moment of self-reflection. He discovers that his smile, "the old burnt-in smile," has disappeared. He recognizes his emptiness and unhappiness. Moreover, he recognizes his lack of formal education, of what he understands to be his essential ignorance. This sense of helplessness, of ineffectuality, of powerlessness, of his utter inability to comprehend what is in books, overwhelms him, and his mind flashes back to a time when he was a child on the seashore "trying to fill a sieve with sand." Montag recalls that, "the faster he poured [the sand], the faster it sifted through with a hot whispering." He now has this same feeling of helplessness as he reads the Bible, open on his lap; his mind seems to be a sieve through which the words pass without Montag's comprehending or remembering them. He knows that in a few hours he must give this precious book to Beatty, and so he attempts to read and memorize the scriptures—in particular, Jesus' Sermon on the Mount. As he attempts to memorize the passages, however, a loud and brassy advertisement for "Denham's Dental Detergent" destroys his concentration.

Montag is trying to rebel, but he is continually frustrated because he has so many mental blocks against non-conformity. He has never before deviated from the norm, and his attempts to establish an individual identity are continually frustrated. Montag's flight to Faber's home is presented as his only hope. The scene reminds one of a man running for his life—which, in fact, he is doing, though he does not fully realize it yet. He is also, though he doesn't know it, already an outcast. He can never return to his former existence. His transformation is ineluctable.

Of significance here is Faber himself, who bears a close resemblance to Carl Jung's archetypal figure of the "old man." According to Jung in his essay "The Phenomenology of the Spirit in Fairy Tales," the old man archetype represents knowledge, reflection, insight, wisdom, cleverness, and intuition on the one hand—and, on the other hand, he represents such moral qualities as good will and readiness to help, which makes his "spiritual" character sufficiently plain. Faber displays these qualities, and symbolic of his spiritual nature, he, like Clarisse, is associated with the color white: "He [Faber] and the white plaster walls inside were much the same. There was white in the flesh of his mouth and his cheeks and his hair was white and his eyes had faded, with white in the vague blueness there."

Faber is a devotee of the ideas contained in books. He is also concerned with the common good of man. Montag senses this immediately and readily admits his feelings of unhappiness and emptiness to Faber. He confesses that the things of value that are missing in his life are books and the truths they teach. For this reason, he asks Faber to teach him to understand what he reads. At first, Faber views this new teaching assignment as a useless, as well as a dangerous, undertaking. This attitude, however, does not deter Faber from launching into this challenging and exciting task.

Besides enlightening Montag, Faber expounds on his philosophy about the use of the books, as well as about society in general. (One can't help but think that Faber's discussion is close to Bradbury's own view, but of course, this is simply speculation.) Faber explains that books have "quality" and "texture," that they reveal stark reality, not only the pleasant aspects of life, but also the bad aspects of life: "They show the pores in the face of life," and their society finds this discomforting. Tragically, society has even begun to program thoughts: people are no longer allowed the leisure time to think for themselves. Faber insists that *leisure* is essential to the proper appreciation of books (by "leisure," Faber does not mean "off hours," the time away from work, but simply ample time to think about things beyond one's self). Distractions, such as the all-encompassing television walls, simply won't allow for it. Ultimately, however, Faber thinks that the truths in books can never be of value in his society again unless its individuals have "the right to carry out actions based on" what is found in the books. Books will be of value only when people are allowed the freedom to act upon what they have learned. On this last point, Faber is pessimistic; he is convinced that this can never happen.

As though in response to Faber's pessimism, Montag presents Faber with an insidious plan, entailing the hiding of books in the homes of firemen so that even *they* will become suspect. Ultimately, through supposed treason, the firehouses themselves will be burned. Faber acknowledges the cleverness of the plan, but he is convinced it will not work because "firemen are rarely necessary." By this he means that "So few want to be rebels anymore." People are too distracted—that is, too "happy"—to want to change things. Cynically, he urges Montag to return home and give up his newly acquired rebelliousness.

This demonstration of cowardice and political nihilism incites Montag to begin ripping pages out of the Bible. Shocked by the destruction of the precious book, Faber, stirred by Montag's rebellious convictions, agrees to help him.

Bradbury later describes this coalition of two as "Montag-plus-Faber, fire plus water." Fire and water images blend, for the product resulting from the union of these two separate and opposite items is a third—wine. Wine looks like water, but it burns like fire. Montag and Faber—together they work, because all is far from well in the world. (The reader might wish to recall Bradbury's comments on the genesis of *Fahrenheit 451* in the introduction.)

As a result of Montag's concern about how he will act when he and Beatty meet next, Faber shows Montag an invention of his—a two-way, Seashell Radio-like communication device that resembles a small "green bullet" and fits in one's ear. Through the use of this device, Faber can be in constant contact with Montag, and he promises to be supportive of him if Beatty attempts to intimidate him. Through the use of Faber's spying invention, they will listen to Captain Beatty together. Faber says that he will be, in effect, "the Queen Bee," remaining safely in the hive; Montag will be "the drone." Before parting, they initiate plans to "[print] a few books, and wait on the war to break the pattern and give us the push we need. A few bombs and the 'families' in the walls of all the homes, like harlequin rats, will shut up!" Perhaps their subversion will restore the public's interest in books. However, despite his decision to help Montag, Faber acknowledges that he is still, ultimately, a coward: he will be safe at home while Montag faces the threat of punishment.

Meanwhile, the threat of war increases. Ten million men have been mobilized, and the people expect victory. The war is a parallel to Montag's attitude concerning his own personal battle. His inner turmoil intensifies. Armed with a friend such as Faber, the two-way "green bullet" radio, and a beginner's knowledge of the true value of books, he is now ready to wage war against Beatty and the rest of his stagnant society.

Montag returns home hoping to talk to Millie, hoping to discuss ideas and books with her. He feels that he is becoming a new man, intoxicated by his new-found inner strength, but his is an idealistic knowledge blended with the zealousness of a convert; he has not considered any sort of pragmatic plan of implementation. Unfortunately, in Montag's case, a little learning is a dangerous thing, for when he returns home, he finds company. Immediately, he launches into a tirade in the presence of two of Millie's friends, Mrs. Phelps and Mrs. Bowles. This tirade will prove costly to his idealistic plans.

Mrs. Phelps and Mrs. Bowles are a good deal like Millie; they are devoted to their television "families," they are politically enervated, and they show little interest in the imminent war. Since their husbands are routinely called away to war, they are unconcerned; it has happened before and may happen again.

Listening to their empty babble, animated by his rebel posture and Faber whispering comfortably in his ear, Montag impulsively disconnects the three-walled television and shouts. "Let's talk." He brings forth a book—which Millie, in a panic, dismisses to the ladies as a fireman's privilege—and begins to read from Matthew Arnold's "Dover Beach":

> Ah, love, let us be true
> To one another! for the world, which seems
> To lie before us like a land of dreams,
> So various, so beautiful, so new,
> Hath really neither joy, nor love, nor light,
> Nor certitude, nor peace, nor help for pain;
> And we are here as on a darkling plain

>Swept with confused alarms of struggle and flight,
>Where ignorant armies clash by night.

Despite their flippancy and chatter, the women—especially Mrs. Phelps—are moved by the poem, though they cannot say why. The Cheshire cat-like smiles that Millie and her friends wear are an indication of the illusion of happiness that they are under. Montag imagines these smiles as "burning" through the walls of the house. Ironically, smiles should signify joy; they do not in this case. They are destructive and perhaps even evil. Further, Millie and her friends are characterized by fire imagery; they light cigarettes and blow the smoke from their mouths. They all have "sun-fired" hair and "blazing" fingernails. They, like the fleet of firemen, are headed toward their own destruction.

Faber attempts, through the two-way radio, to calm Montag's zealous anger. He urges Montag to make believe, to say that he is joking, and Faber commands him to throw his book of poems into the incinerator. Despite Faber's admonitions and Millie's defensive maneuvers, Montag continues, soundly cursing both Mrs. Phelps and Mrs. Bowles for their empty and corrupt lives. Mrs. Bowles leaves in a fury, Mrs. Phelps in tears. Characteristically, Millie escapes from this horrible scene by rushing to the bathroom and downing several sleeping pills. She wants to sleep and forget. Montag, "exhausted and bewildered with himself," hides several of the remaining books in some bushes in his backyard, then goes off to work, carrying with him a substitute book to give to Beatty in the place of the Bible he left with Faber.

Montag, as well he might, dreads the meeting with Beatty, even though Faber promises to be with him via the two-way radio implanted in Montag's ear. Captain Beatty's suspicion of Montag steadily increases as he watches Montag with an "alcohol-flame stare." He tries to coax Montag into admitting his crime of stealing (and reading) books, but Faber is true to his word and supports Montag during Beatty's taunting. In a most striking diatribe, Beatty is revealed to be extremely well read; he quotes, accurately, authors from a wide range of historical periods and is able to apply what he has read. He has obviously thought about what the works mean, and, in a curious way, uses them to good effect against Montag. He is aware of Montag's new-found zealousness ("Read a few lines and off you go over the cliff. Bang, you're ready to blow up the

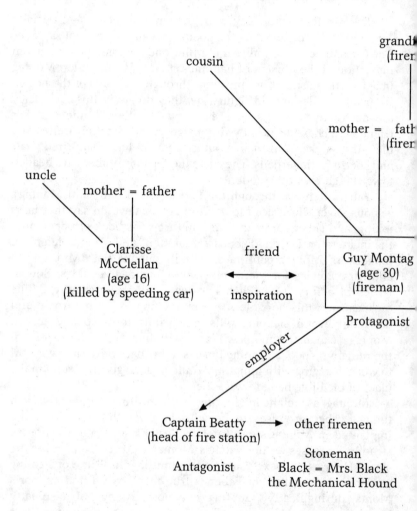

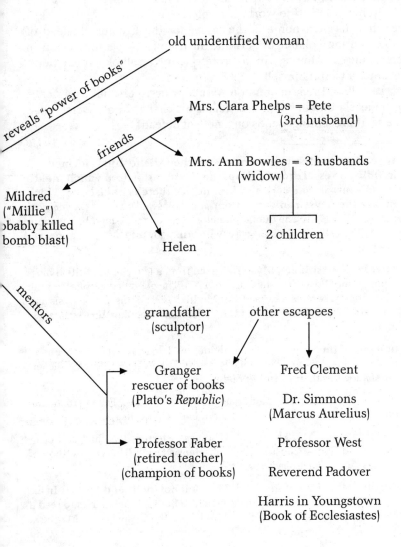

old unidentified woman

reveals "power of books"

friends

Mrs. Clara Phelps = Pete
(3rd husband)

Mrs. Ann Bowles = 3 husbands
(widow)

2 children

Mildred
("Millie")
ɔbably killed
bomb blast)

Helen

mentors

grandfather
(sculptor)

other escapees

Granger
rescuer of books
(Plato's *Republic*)

Fred Clement

Dr. Simmons
(Marcus Aurelius)

Professor Faber
(retired teacher)
(champion of books)

Professor West

Reverend Padover

Harris in Youngstown
(Book of Ecclesiastes)

world, chop off heads, knock down women and children, destroy authority") and even manages to urge Montag in a direction which would cause him to abandon his recently acquired humanistic convictions.

Before Montag can respond to Beatty's tirade (no doubt his rebuttal would have failed miserably), the fire alarm sounds, and the firemen rush off to work. In a colossal act of irony, Montag realizes that his own home is the target for the firemen. Instead of implementing a plan to undermine the firemen by planting books in their houses, Montag, in a grotesque reversal of expectations, becomes a victim himself.

Part Two, then, centers on Montag's first personal experience with ideas found in books and details his change into a social rebel. The section seemingly ends on a note of defeat.

- **We cannot tell the precise moment when friendship is formed. As in filling a vessel drop by drop, there is at last a drop which makes it run over; so in a series of kindnesses there is at last one which makes the heart run over** from James Boswell's *Life of Dr. Johnson*, published in 1791. The quotation helps Montag understand his relationship with the mysterious Clarisse, who brings joy into his life for no obvious reason.

- **That favorite subject. Myself.** taken from a letter of the British biographer James Boswell, dated July 16, 1763. The quotation emphasizes the chasm that separates Montag from Mildred, who shuns self-analysis and submerges herself in drugs and the television programs that sedate her mind.

- **half out of the cave** Bradbury alludes to Plato's cave allegory, found in Book 7 of his *Republic*. The analogy describes how people rely on flickering shadows as their source of reality.

- **Faber** the character's name suggests that of Peter Faber (1506–45), tutor of Ignatius Loyola and founder of two Jesuit colleges.

- **Mr. Jefferson? Mr. Thoreau?** Thomas Jefferson, the chief author of the United States Constitution, and Henry David Thoreau, author of *Walden* and *Civil Disobedience*.

- **Consider the lilies of the field. They toil not, neither do they** In his surreal dash on the subway toward Faber's house, Montag tries to read a line from Jesus' Sermon on the Mount from the Gospel of St. Matthew. The line, which is taken from Chapter 6, verses 28–29, concludes, "And yet I say unto you, that even Solomon in all his glory was not arrayed like one of these." This quotation reminds Montag that spiritual hunger is greater than material need.

- **Caesar's praetorian guard** a reference to the bodyguards that surrounded the Roman Caesars, beginning with Rome's first emperor, Octavian, later named Augustus. While holding back the mob, the praetorians wielded supreme control over the rulers they sought to protect and are thought to have assassinated Caligula and replaced him with Claudius, a crippled historian who was their choice of successor.

- **The salamander devours its tail** Faber, who creates a way to implicate firemen in their own menace and therefore eradicate them, characterizes his plot with an image of self-destruction.

- **this electronic cowardice** Faber, an old man who is too fearful to confront Captain Beatty, is willing to direct Montag's confrontation through his electronic listening and speaking device.

- **The Book of Job** Faber selects a book of the Old Testament which describes how Job is tested by God. The upshot of Job's struggle with suffering, loss, and temptation is that he learns to trust.

- **Vesuvius** a volcano near Naples which erupted August 24, 79 A.D., burying the citizens of Pompeii and Herculaneum.

- **Cheshire Cat** a grinning character from Chapter 6 of Lewis Carroll's *Alice in Wonderland*.

- **In again out again Finnegan** a common nonsense rhyme indicating Mrs. Phelps' lack of concern about the war and her husband's part in it. The quotation restates "Off again, on again, gone again, Finnegan," a terse telegram about a rail crash from Finnegan, a railroad boss, to Flanagan, his employer.

- **Dover Beach** Although Mildred makes the choice of what her husband should read, Matthew Arnold's poem typifies Montag's pessimism as he tries to fathom the vapid, purposeless lifestyles of the three women. The poem forces the women to respond—Mrs. Phelps with tears and Mrs. Bowles with anger.

- **fire plus water** Montag, who perceives the split halves of his being, anticipates the distillation of his fiery self into wine after Faber has molded his intellect with wisdom and teaching.

- **Who are a little wise, the best fools be** a line from John Donne's poem "The Triple Fool," which Beatty uses to confuse and stifle Montag.

- **the sheep returns to the fold. We're all sheep who have strayed at times** Beatty alludes to the prophecy in Isaiah 53:6: "All we like sheep have gone astray; we have turned every one to his own way; and the Lord hath laid on him the iniquity of us all." The implied message is that Montag has betrayed his fellow firemen.

- **Truth is truth, to the end of reckoning** Beatty's montage of quotations rambles on to a verse from Shakespeare's *Measure for Measure*, Act V, Scene i, line 45.

- **They are never alone that are accompanied with noble thoughts** a verse taken from Sir Philip Sidney's *Arcadia*, which in turn paraphrases a line from Beaumont and Fletcher's *Love's Cure*, Act III, Scene iii.

- **Sweet food of sweetly uttered knowledge** a line from Sir Philip Sidney's *Defense of Poesy*.

- **Words are like leaves and where they most abound, Much fruit of sense beneath is rarely found** Beatty quotes a couplet from Alexander Pope's *Essay on Criticism* as cynical commentary on his profusely garbled and contradictory recitation.

- **A little learning is a dangerous thing. Drink deep, or taste not the Pierian spring; There shallow draughts intoxicate the brain, and drinking largely sobers us again** a famous pair of couplets from Alexander Pope's *Essay on Criticism*, which warns the learner that scholarship requires dedication for maximum effect.

- **Knowledge is more than equivalent to force** an aphorism from Chapter 13 of Dr. Samuel Johnson's *Rasselas*.

- **He is no wise man that will quit a certainty for an uncertainty** an aphorism from Dr. Samuel Johnson's *Idler*.

- **Truth will come to light, murder will not be hid long!** from Shakespeare's *Merchant of Venice*, Act II, Scene ii, Line 86.

- **Oh God, he speaks only of his horse** a paraphrase of "he doth nothing but talk of his horse" from Shakespeare's *Merchant of Venice*, Act I, Scene ii, Lines 37–38.

- **The Devil can cite Scripture for his purpose** from Shakespeare's *Merchant of Venice*, Act I, Scene iii, Line 99.

- **This age thinks better of a gilded fool, than of a threadbare saint in wisdom's school** a couplet from Thomas Dekker's *Old Fortunatus*.

- **The dignity of truth is lost with much protesting** a line from Ben Jonson's *Catiline's Conspiracy*, Act III, Scene ii.

- **Carcasses bleed at the sight of the murderer**   a line from Robert Burton's *Anatomy of Melancholy*, Part I, Section I, Member 2, Subsection 5.

- **trench mouth**   severe ulceration of the gums, tonsils, and mucous membranes of the mouth resulting from bacterial infection.

- **Knowledge is power**   a line from Francis Bacon's *Advancement of Learning*, Book I, i, 3.

- **A dwarf on a giant's shoulders sees the furthest of the two**   from *Democritus to the Reader*, Robert Burton's paraphrase from Lucan's *Civil War*, which is echoed in Sir Isaac Newton's letter to Robert Hooke, February 5, 1675 or 1676.

- **The folly of mistaking a metaphor for a proof, a torrent of verbiage for a spring of capital truths, and oneself as an oracle is inborn in us**   a paraphrase of Paul Valery's *Introduction to the Method of Leonardo da Vinci*.

- **A kind of excellent dumb discourse**   a line from Shakespeare's *Tempest*, Act III, Scene iii, Line 38.

- **All's well that is well in the end**   a paraphrase of Shakespeare's *All's Well That Ends Well*, Act IV, Scene iv, Line 35.

- **the tyranny of the majority**   from John Emerich Edward Dalberg-Acton's *History of Freedom and Other Essays*.

PART III: BURNING BRIGHT

The ironies begin to multiply as Montag discovers that it was Millie herself who turned in the fire alarm. While Beatty seems to regret what he must do, he taunts Montag in a mean-spirited way: "Old Montag wanted to fly near the sun and now that he's burnt his damn wings, he wonders why. Didn't I hint enough when I sent the Hound around your place?" Though our sympathies are, rightly so, with Montag, Beatty is revealed here as a man torn between duty and conscience, which makes him more of an individual and less a villain, less a straw man. He doesn't particularly want to arrest Montag for breaking the law, and his metaphorical concept of Montag as Icarus further reveals his active imagination and knowledge of (illegal) books.

Yet it is through sheer maliciousness that Beatty forces Montag to set fire to the house. Little does he realize that Montag finds a certain perverse satisfaction in torching the television screens: "And then he came to the parlor where the great idiot monsters lay asleep with their white thoughts and their snowy dreams. And he shot a bolt at each of the three blank walls and the vacuum hissed out at him." In a strange way, Montag gets his revenge on the television screens that he hates so strongly.

The entire episode has, for Montag, a phantasmagorical quality. He perceives his arrival and the preparations for the burning as a "carnival" being set up; later, after the destruction of his house and after the spectators have disappeared, it's as if "the great tents of the circus had slumped into charcoal and rubble and the show was well over." After this burning, Montag is not smiling.

Meanwhile, Faber urges Montag to escape, but Montag is hesitant because the Mechanical Hound is on the prowl. It is not surprising that, momentarily, Montag lapses into his former way of thinking as a result of Beatty's verbal assaults and his discovery of the "green bullet."

Beatty is unrelenting, to be sure. Not only is Beatty convinced he can track the two-way radio to its source (Faber), but he also reduces Montag's book knowledge to so much posturing: "Why don't you belch Shakespeare at me, you fumbling snob? . . . Go ahead now, you secondhand literateur, pull the trigger." With the flame thrower in his hand and, in his mind, the seeming futility of ever correcting the ills of society, Montag decides that fire, after all, is probably the best solution for everything. "We never burned *right*," he says.

The meaning of Montag's utterance is open to speculation. At first glance, it is a statement about passion: if the firemen have to burn, they should know what it is that they are burning. They should know what the subjects of the books are and what they contain. Or, possibly, burning shouldn't be done simply as a mindless job that one does by rote, but done out of political and ideological convictions. Given the context, however, he says it with the implication that Beatty was wrong to encourage burning when he, Beatty, knew the value of the books.

At any rate, he turns the liquid fire full on Captain Beatty, who collapses to the pavement like a "charred wax doll." Beatty had always preached to Montag that fire was the solution to all of one's problems. "Don't face a problem, burn it," Beatty had told him. It is no wonder—and also superb poetic justice—that Beatty is burned as a solution to Montag's problem. Note once again, in describing Beatty's death, that Bradbury uses the image of a wax doll. Beatty has been charred and destroyed by the fire that gave purpose and direction to his life.

After cold-cocking Stoneman and Black, Montag is about to escape, but the Mechanical Hound stuns him in the leg with its procaine needle. In just a few short moments, Montag has become a criminal, an enemy of the people. He now becomes a hunted man, sought by the police and the firemen's salamanders. The police, he is sure, with the aid of helicopters, will immediately begin a manhunt. He has no friend to turn to but Faber. It is only Faber who holds some promise of hope for survival.

Despite the urgency, Montag rescues some of the books he had hidden in his back yard (Millie had burned most of them, but had missed a few). As he stumbles off down the alley, a sudden and awesome recognition stops him cold in his tracks: "In the middle of the crying Montag knew it for the truth. Beatty had wanted to die. He had just stood there, not really trying to save himself, just stood there, joking, needling, thought Montag, and the thought was enough to stifle his sobbing and let him pause for air." This is a most curious moment for both the reader and for Montag, for suddenly we understand Beatty in a much different way. What Montag had always imagined, that all firemen were happy, has no basis now—neither he nor Beatty was happy. Beatty's cynicism masked an imaginative mind stifled by a society that had outlawed individual thinking and put a premium on conformity. Beatty was a man who understood his own compromised morality and who privately admired the conviction of people like Montag.

In a strange way, Beatty had wanted to commit suicide, but evidently had been too cowardly to carry it out. The general unhappiness and despondency of certain members of society have been illustrated three times before this last incident: Millie's near-suicide with the overdose of sleeping pills ("We get these cases nine or ten a night," the attendant had told Montag), the oblique reference to the fireman in Seattle, who "purposely set a Mechanical Hound to his own chemical complex and let it loose," and the unidentified woman who chose to be immolated with her books. People in Montag's society are simply not happy. Their desire for death reflects a social malaise of meaninglessness and purposelessness.

On his way to Faber's house, Montag discovers that war has been declared. This hint of doom, which has been looming on the horizon during the entire novel, is now reaching a climax. This new development again serves as a parallel to the situation in which Montag finds himself.

As Montag runs, his wounded leg feels like a "chunk of burnt pine log" that he is forced to carry "as a penance for some obscure sin." Once more, the imagery of fire is used to suggest purification. The penance Montag must pay here is the result of all the years of destruction while he was a fireman. Even though the pain in his leg is excruciating, he must overcome even more daunting obstacles before he achieves redemption.

In his journey to Faber's, Montag confronts an unforeseen danger: crossing a boulevard. Because the automobiles travel at such high speeds, it makes crossing the street extremely dangerous—coupled by the fact that because such little value is given to a person's life, it has become a sport to run over pedestrians. (Recall that Clarisse was killed by a hit-and-run driver.) In Montag's case, the danger is compounded because he has a crippled leg, deadened with procaine: "The boulevard was as clean as the surface of an arena two minutes before the appearance of certain unnamed victims and certain unknown killers."

Despite the danger, Montag has little choice; he must cross the boulevard in order to reach Faber. Either he must risk crossing the boulevard or face certain execution in a matter of minutes. The "beetles," or automobiles, travel at such high speeds that they are likened to bullets fired from invisible rifles. Fire imagery is enlisted to describe these "beetles": their headlights seem to burn Montag's cheeks and, as one of them bears down on him, it seems to become "a torch hurtling upon him." A fortuitous stumble allows Montag to escape certain death, so, unharmed (except for one-sixteenth of an inch of black tire tread on his middle finger), he travels onward.

Montag makes one stop prior to his arrival at Faber's home. He stops at the home of a fellow fireman—Black's house—and hides the books that he's been carrying in the kitchen. He reasons that since Black has been responsible for burning many other people's homes, it is now his turn to have his own home burned. In so doing, he activates the plan which he had previously sketched for Faber. He phones a fire alarm then waits until he hears the sirens before he continues on to Faber's. Black's house will be burned.

Together, Montag and Faber make their plans for escape. Faber tells Montag to try for the river. If he can cross it, he should then make his way down the railroad tracks leading out of the city, far enough to meet up with one of the many groups of exiles forced to flee to the countryside. He will find refuge with them. As for himself, Faber plans to catch the early morning bus to St. Louis to get in touch with an old printer friend of his. He, too, intends to risk his life to insure the immortality of books.

While the two men make their plans, the television announces that a massive manhunt has been organized to track down Montag. They discover that a new Mechanical Hound has been brought in to aid in the search and that the networks intend to participate by televising the chase. Montag, rightly so, imagines the manhunt as a "game" and as a "circus" that "must go on," and finally as a "one-man carnival." This is not to say that Montag imagines it as something which is silly or playful, but that everyday experience is rendered as a spectacle.

With the news that a second Mechanical Hound has been brought to the area, Faber and Montag must take careful, precautionary steps in order to avoid capture. Montag instructs Faber to burn in the incinerator everything that he, Montag, has touched and then to rub everything else down with alcohol. He suggests that Faber cover the scent with moth spray, then hose off the sidewalks and turn on the lawn sprinklers. In this way, they can confuse the Mechanical Hound's sense of smell and cause him to lose Montag's trail *into* Faber's house; Faber will remain safe while Montag lures the Hound to the river. Before he leaves, he takes a cardboard valise filled with some old clothes of Faber's, as well as a bottle of whiskey. Montag makes a run for the river, knowing that the Mechanical Hound is still on his trail even as helicopters gather and hover overhead.

Montag finally hobbles to the safety of the river undetected, where he douses himself in whiskey and dresses in Faber's clothes. After discarding the valise, he plunges into the river and is borne away. He is "three hundred yards downstream" when the Mechanical Hound loses his scent at the river's edge. Undaunted, however, the police refuse to be denied the capture, and the "lights switched back to land, the helicopters swerved over the city again, as if they had picked up another trail."

They cannot allow the public to know of their failure, so they enact a hoax: an innocent man is chosen as a victim for the TV cameras. The populace is deceived into thinking that Montag is dead because their wall televisions actually depict the murder of a man, even though this man is not Montag (whom the populace, of course, has never seen).

While the chase is continuing elsewhere, Montag floats in the river toward the far shore and safety. The imagery of water, a traditional symbol of regeneration and renewal (and, for Carl Jung, transformation), coupled with Montag's putting on of Faber's clothes, suggests that the tale of transformation is complete. Montag has become an outlaw and a rebel in just a few short days.

His time spent in the water, accompanied by the escape from the city, serves as a kind of epiphany for Montag's spirit: "For the first time in a dozen years [that is, since he became a fireman] the stars were coming out above him, in great processions of wheeling fire." The escape allows him—again, for the first time in years—to *think*. He thinks about his dual roles as man and as fireman. "After a long time of floating on the land and a short time of floating in the river," we are told, "he knew why he must never burn again in his life." Only human beings are capable of making choices (and hence, are moral), and his moral choice is to cease burning.

Montag emerges from the river transformed. Now in the country, strong melancholic emotions are stirred by his first tactile sensation—that of "the dry smell of hay blowing from some distant field." Though Montag may be a man who has trouble articulating his feelings, we learn that he is a man of deep feelings. The entire episode of his leaving the river and entering the country is evocative of a spiritual transformation. He has sad thoughts of Millie, who is somewhere back in the city, and has a sensuous fantasy of Clarisse; both of them are now associated with the city and a life that he no longer lives, and to which he can never return.

Where the city has been metaphorically associated with a stifling and oppressive technology, the country is a place of unbounded possibility, which at first terrifies Montag: "He was crushed by darkness and the look of the country and the million odors on a wind that iced the body." In his earlier life, recall that

Montag could smell only kerosene, which was "nothing but perfume" to him. The forest into which he stumbles is rampant with life; he imagines "a billion leaves on the land" and is overcome by the natural odors with which he is confronted.

To underscore the strangeness of the environment Montag has entered, Bradbury has him stumble across a railroad track which had, for Montag, "a familiarity." He is, ironically, more familiar with an environment composed of concrete and steel than he is with grass and trees. Since he is most familiar (and comfortable) with something associated with urban life (the railroad tracks), he remembers that Faber told him to follow them, "the single familiar thing, the magic charm he might need a little while, to touch, to feel beneath his feet" as he moves on.

Half an hour later, he sees a fire in the black distance. To signal the profound change that Montag has undergone, we learn now that he sees the fire as "strange" because, "It was not burning, it was *warming*." This is not a fire which destroys, but heals, and by so doing, it draws Montag to the company of his fellow outcasts, book burners of a different sort.

The leader of these outcasts is Granger, a former author and intellectual. Curiously, Granger seems to have expected Montag and reveals his good will by offering Montag "a small bottle of colorless fluid," which is intended to "change the chemical index" of Montag's perspiration; after Montag drinks the fluid, the Mechanical Hound will no longer be able to track him. Not only is Montag garbed in clothes that are not his, the chemical which Granger offers now changes his perspiration. Montag has become, literally, a different man.

Granger explains to Montag the nature of the commune and how each member chooses a book and memorizes it. When the entire book has been memorized, it is then burned to prevent the individual from being arrested by the authorities. From that time on, it is transmitted verbally from one generation to another.

Montag confesses to Granger that he had once memorized some of the Book of Ecclesiastes. Granger tells him that a man named Harris knows those verses from memory, but if anything ever happens to Harris, Montag will become that book. Now, not only has Montag learned the value of a book, but he has also learned that he can "become the book" itself.

When Montag admits the grand failure of his plan of planting books in firemen's houses, Granger replies that the plan might have worked had it been carried out on a national scale. He feels, however, that the commune's way of giving everlasting life to books through their embodiment in people is the best way. Each individual becomes precious in his or her own way: "We are model citizens, in our own special way," Granger says.

Ironically, Montag and Granger do their talking around a fire that is warming rather than destructive. With Granger and others, Montag gains a sense of warmth, of personal well-being, and recovers a sense of faith in the future. He is gaining an understanding of the fire of spirit, of life, and of immortality, and forgetting the fire that destroys. Notice that when the campfire is no longer necessary, every man lends a hand to help put it out. This action is further proof of the things Granger has been telling Montag: group effort is necessary if a positive goal is ever to be reached.

Because of war which could begin at any minute, the commune is forced to move south, farther down the river, away from the city that is a sure target of attack. Jets shriek overhead continually, heading for battle. Montag associates Millie with the city, but admits to Granger that, strangely, he doesn't "feel much of anything" for her. That part of his life, as well as everything having to do with the city, seems distant and unreal. He feels sorry for her because he intuitively knows that she will probably be killed in the war. He is ashamed because in all their years together, he was able to offer her nothing.

While Granger and Montag talk, jet planes fly over the distant city, releasing bombs. With an abrupt finale, the city is destroyed: "as quick as the whisper of a scythe the war was finished." The city is reduced to rubble. Montag's thoughts turn to Millie, and he imagines how the last moments of life must have been for her. He pictures her looking at her wall television set. In an instant, the television screen goes blank, and Millie is left seeing only a mirror image of herself. Montag imagines that just before her death, Millie finally sees and knows for herself just how superficial and empty her life has been. And in that instant, Montag recalls when he met her: "A long time ago," in Chicago. His former life seems only a dream.

A new day begins, and a fire providing warmth and heat for cooking has been made. Granger looks into the fire and realizes its life-giving quality as he utters the word "phoenix." The phoenix, he says, was "a silly damn bird" which "every few hundred years" built a pyre "and burned himself up." Granger imagines the bird as "first cousin to Man" because the bird was continually going through rebirth only to destroy himself again. The mythology of fire surrounding this ancient bird is strategic to the lessons of this book.

Bradbury alludes to this bird repeatedly in the novel. The firemen wear an emblem of the Phoenix on their chests; Beatty wears the sign of the phoenix on his hat and drives a phoenix car. When Beatty is burned to death, his death by fire prepares for a rebirth that is traditionally symbolized by the phoenix sign. Montag's destruction of Beatty ultimately results in his escape from the city and his meeting Granger. All these actions have led to a rebirth into a new and vital life. Montag's new life is filled with hope and the promise of a new era of humanism, depicted in the words Montag recalls from the Bible: "To everything there is a season. A time to break down, a time to build up."

Shaken by the destruction of the city, Granger, Montag and the rest are compelled to return to the city and lend what help they can. It is a curious moment, but characteristic of Bradbury. In his novel *The Martian Chronicles*, for example, people flee the Earth and head for Mars because they are sure that Earth is going to be destroyed in a nuclear holocaust. However, when the transplanted Earth people hear that the holocaust has indeed occurred, they return to Earth immediately because they know it no longer exists as they remember it. This movement is repeated at the conclusion of this story. Montag flees the city only to return to it after its destruction. While altruistically compelled to lend aid to the survivors (of which there must have been very few), there seems to be some ritualistic need for Montag (and the others) to return to the city from which they escaped. Though they have had to escape the city for political reasons, its familiarity nonetheless remains psychologically comforting. The implication would seem to be that in the death of someone or something that one fiercely hates, one has also lost an essential part of one's identity.

Fahrenheit 451 is explicit in its warnings and moral lessons aimed at the present. Bradbury believes that our social organization can easily become oppressive and regimented unless it changes its present course of suppression of an individual's innate rights through censorship. The degenerated future depicted in *Fahrenheit 451* represents the culmination of dangerous tendencies that are submerged in our own society. At the very least, the book asserts that the freedom of the imagination is a corollary of individual freedom.

The title which Bradbury gives to Part Three alludes to William Blake's poem "The Tyger." This poem, from Blake's *Songs of Innocence and Experience*, is often interpreted as a meditation about the origin of evil in the world. The first four lines of the poem are:

> Tyger, Tyger, burning bright,
> In the forests of the night:
> What immortal hand or eye,
> Could frame thy fearful symmetry?

In Blake's poem, the tiger is often considered a symbol for a world in which evil is at work; it speaks also of the dual nature of all existence. Appropriately, Part Three's title, "Burning Bright," serves a dual function: it summarizes the situation at the conclusion of the book, for even while the city is still burning brightly from the war's destruction, the spirit of the commune is also brightly burning, signifying a future of hope and optimism.

- **Burning Bright** The heading derives from "The Tyger," a poem by William Blake, discussed above.

- **Old Montag wanted to fly near the sun and now that he's burnt his damn wings, he wonders why** Beatty alludes to Icarus, the son of Daedalus, an inventor in Greek mythology. After Daedalus makes wings and teaches his son to fly, he warns the boy not to go too near the sun. Icarus, intrigued with the power of flight, fails to heed the warning, the wax melts which holds the wings together, and he drowns in the sea below.

- **You think you can walk on water** Beatty alludes to Jesus walking on water, as recorded in Mark 6:45–51.

- **There is no terror, Cassius, in your threats, for I am arm'd so strong in honesty that they pass by me as an idle wind, which I respect not** Beatty taunts Montag with a passage from Shakespeare's *Julius Caesar*, Act IV, Scene iii, Line 66.

- **there's lots of old Harvard degrees on the tracks** Faber refers to the educated people who have dropped out of sight to live the hobo life outside the city.

- **Keystone Comedy**   From 1914 to 1920, director Mack Sennett and Keystone Studios produced a series of madcap silent film comedies featuring the Keystone Cops.

- **the guild of the asbestos-weaver**   Montag associates his desire to stop the burning with the formation of a new trade union. Like the guilds of the Middle Ages, the asbestos-weavers symbolize progress against the tyranny of the past.

- **coat of a thousand colors**   Granger alludes to Joseph, the character in Genesis 37:3–4 who receives a long-sleeved, ornamental coat of many colors from Jacob, his doting father. The coat, symbolizing favoritism shown by Jacob toward his son, alienates the other sons, who sell their brother to passing traders, stain the coat with goat's blood, and return it to their father to prove that a wild animal has eaten Joseph.

- **crying in the wilderness**   Granger compares his group's minority status to John the Baptist, the prophet whom Isaiah predicted would one day announce the coming of the Messiah (Isaiah 40:3-5).

- **V-2 rocket**   the Germans' use of the first long-range, liquid-fuel missile carrying a ton of explosives during World War II changed the face of modern warfare.

- **atom-bomb mushroom**   On August 6, 1945, over Hiroshima, Japan, American pilots dropped the first atomic bomb to be used in war. The explosion, which rose in a straight column two hundred miles high, ballooned outward like a huge mushroom.

- **I hate a Roman named Status Quo!**   Granger's grandfather made a pun out of the Latin phrase, which means the situation as it now exists.

- **whisper of a scythe**   In an extended metaphor which begins with a giant hand sowing the grains of bombs over the land, the image concludes with the death-dealing scythe, the symbol carried in the hand of Father time, an image of death, which cuts down life in a single, silent sweep.

- **To everything there is a season**   Montag recalls an often-quoted segment of Ecclesiastes 3:1–8, which reminds him that there is a time for dying as well as a time for living.

- **And on either side of the river was there a tree of life, which bare twelve manner of fruits, and yielded her fruit every month; and the leaves of the tree are for the healing of the nations**   a prophecy from verse two of Revelation 22, the last book in the Bible.

CHARACTER ANALYSES

GUY MONTAG

Guy Montag, the novel's **protagonist**, having followed the tradition begun by his grandfather and father, takes pride in his job with the fire department. He fits the stereotypical role, with his "black hair, black brows . . . fiery face, and . . . blue-steel shaved but unshaved look." A model of twenty-fourth century professionalism, he reeks of cinders and ash and enjoys dressing in his uniform, playing the role of a symphony conductor as he directs the brass nozzle toward illegal books, and smelling the kerosene which raises the temperature to the required 451 degrees Fahrenheit, the temperature at which book paper ignites. In his first eight years of employment, Montag had even joined in the firemen's bestial sport of setting small animals loose and betting on which ones the Mechanical Hound would annihilate first.

The last two years, however, have witnessed a growing discontent in Montag, a "fireman turned sour" who cannot yet name the cause of his emptiness and disaffection. He characterizes his restless mind as "full of bits and pieces"; he requires sedatives to sleep. His hands, more attuned to his inner workings than his conscious mind, seem to take charge of his behavior. Daily, he returns to a loveless, meaningless marriage, symbolized by his cold bedroom furnished with twin beds. Drawn to the lights and conversation of the McClellan family next door, he forces himself to remain at home, yet watches them through the French windows.

Through friendship with Clarisse McClellan, Montag perceives the harshness of society as opposed to the joys of nature, of which he rarely partakes. When Clarisse teases him about not being in love, he experiences a **coming to knowledge** and sinks into a despair which characterizes most of the novel. He suffers guilt for secreting books behind the hall ventilator grille and for failing to love his wife, whom he cannot even remember meeting for the first time. Yet, even though he harbors no affection for Mildred, Montag shudders at the impersonal, mechanized medical care which restores his dying wife to health.

Montag's moroseness reaches a critical point after he witnesses the immolation of an old woman, who willingly embraces death when firemen come to burn her books. His **psychosomatic** illness, a significant mix of chills and fever, fails to fool his employer, who easily identifies the cause of Montag's malaise—a dangerously expanded sensibility in a world which prizes a dulled consciousness. Lured by books, Montag forces Mildred to join him in reading. His hunger for **humanistic** knowledge drives him to Professor Faber, the one educated person whom he feels he can trust to teach him.

Following the burning of the old woman, his company's first human victim, Montag faces an agonizing spiritual **dilemma** of love and hate for his job. Ironically, although, as a fireman, he is marked by the phoenix symbol, he is inhibited from rising like the fabled bird because he lacks the know-how to transform intellectual growth into deeds. It is only after he contacts Faber that the **metamorphosis** begins, signifying his rebirth as the phoenix of a new generation. A duality evolves, the blend of himself and Faber, his **alter ego** With Faber's help, Montag weathers the transformation and returns to his job to confront Captain Beatty, his **nemesis**. Beatty classifies Montag's problem as an intense **romanticism**, actualized by contact with Clarisse. Pulled back and forth between Faber's words from the listening device in his ear and the cynical sneers and gibes of Beatty, who cites lines from so many works of literature that he dazzles his adversary, Montag moves blindly to the fire truck when an alarm sounds. Beatty, who rarely drives, takes the wheel and propels the fire truck toward the next target—Montag's house.

When Beatty prepares to arrest him, Montag realizes that he cannot contain his loathing for a sadistic, escapist society. Momentarily contemplating the consequences of his act, he ignites Beatty and watches him burn. As Montag races away from the lurid scene, he at first suffers a wave of remorse, then concludes that Beatty maneuvered him into the killing. Resourceful and courageous, Montag outwits the Mechanical Hound, but, impaired by a numbed leg, he is nearly run over by a carful of murderous teenage joyriders. With Faber's help, he embraces his budding idealism and accepts on faith the hope of escape into a better life, one in which dissent and discussion will redeem humanity from their gloomy Dark Age.

Baptized to a new life by his plunge into the river and dressed in Faber's clothes, Montag flees the draconian society, which is fated to suffer a brief, annihilating attack. The cataclysm forces him face-down onto the earth, where he experiences a disjointed remembrance of his courtship ten years earlier. Just as his leg recovers its feeling, Montag's humanity returns. After Granger helps him accept the destruction of the city and the probable annihilation of Mildred, Montag looks forward to a time when people and books can again flourish.

CAPTAIN BEATTY

A satanic presence enshrouded in "thunderheads of tobacco smoke," Captain Beatty, the shrewd, ruthless **antagonist** of the story, is linked repeatedly to fire, which ultimately kills him, and the fates, as represented by recurrent card games. As leader of a fire company, he hosts an unwholesome camaraderie with the bureaucratized book burners who follow his orders. Symbolically, he drives a "yellow-flame-colored beetle with . . . black, char-colored tires." Like the Mechanical Hound, he noses out information, such as the pattern of disloyalty in firemen, Montag's relationship with Clarisse, and the presence of books in Montag's house. He remains attuned to the idiosyncrasies of his men and is not deceived by Montag's feigned illness. His authoritarian nature surfaces in his terse order to Mildred to turn off her screens and to Guy to return to work later in the shift.

A malicious, destructive phoenix fire chief, Beatty is an educated, perceptive manipulator who surrounds himself with a nest of literary snippets. From this mishmash of **aphorisms**, he selects appropriate weapons with which to needle and vex Montag, his adversary, in a one-sided verbal duel. Beatty's stand against the dissenting fireman is an essential outgrowth of his role as the sole phoenix of his dark world. At Montag's bedside and later in front of his house, Beatty overestimates his control of a desperate man. When Montag sets him aflame, Beatty burns into black ash, opening the way for Montag to spring into his own incarnation as the succeeding phoenix and bringer of light.

CLARISSE McCLELLAN

A lover of life and nature, Clarisse, an affable neighbor who is nearing her seventeenth birthday, is the **foil** of Mildred, Montag's cold, mindless, conforming wife. Delightfully human and aware of her surroundings, Clarisse disdains the "fact learning" that passes for modern education. She enjoys rain, dandelions, autumn leaves, and even sessions with her analyst, who misdiagnoses her exuberance for living. Powered by an insatiable curiosity, Clarisse, whom Beatty labels a "time bomb," serves as the catalyst that impels Montag toward a painful, but necessary self-examination. With gentle pricks to his self-awareness, Clarisse reveals to him the absence of love, pleasure, and contentment in his life. Her role in the novel is only the forerunner of the spiritual revitalization completed by Faber and Granger. Her terrible death, nearly repeated when a careening vehicle passes over the tip of Montag's finger, underscores the rampant dehumanization of society and the resulting random acts of violence.

PROFESSOR FABER

Quavering on the brink of rebellion against the casual drift of society from **humanism** to oppression, Professor Faber, a bloodless, white-haired academic who protects his "peanut-brittle bones" and castigates himself for his "terrible cowardice," represents a sterling redeeming quality—a belief in the integrity of the individual. He reveres the magic in literature, which "stitched the patches of the universe into one garment for us." Because he is over twice Montag's age, Faber, forced into exile forty years earlier, provides the look backward which enables the hero to see how a literate society allowed itself to slide into mechanization and repression. Willing to read books, discuss philosophies, and enable his disciple to escape the avenging **dystopia**, Faber is reduced to a soothing, insightful, cajoling voice in Montag's ear. After the listening device falls into Beatty's hands, Faber, invigorated by his contact with Montag, takes the 5 A.M. bus from the disintegrating city toward St. Louis, where he hopes to produce books with a fellow bibliophile.

MILDRED MONTAG

Mildred, Montag's wife whom he courted in Chicago and married when they were both twenty, is a study in shallowness and mediocrity. Her abnormally white flesh and chemically burnt hair epitomize a society that demands an artificial beauty in women through diets and hair dye. Completely immersed in an electronic world and growing more incompatible with Montag with every electronic gadget that enters her house, she fills her waking hours with manic drives in the beetle and a TV clown, who distracts her from her real feelings, which lead her nearly to suicide from a drug overdose. Unwilling and unable to analyze rationally, she lives the shallow life that Beatty touts—acquiescence to a technological chamber of horrors. She distances herself from real emotion by identifying with "the family," a three-dimensional fiction in which she plays a scripted part. Her longing for a fourth wall of television makes one wonder how deeply she is capable of submerging **fantasy** to withdraw from the roles of wife, mother, and whole human being.

Addicted to the labor-saving machines that toast and butter her bread and fill her mind with simplistic entertainment, she forgets to bring aspirin to her ailing husband and recedes into monosyllabic communication. Her replies to him are impersonal and callous, as illustrated by her bland announcement of Clarisse's death. To remove any doubts about her materialistic, robotic lifestyle, Mildred surrounds herself with friends like Clara Phelps and Ann Bowles, both vapid and witless dullards who select a presidential candidate by his televised good looks. It is not surprising that Mildred is able to betray her husband and flee their marriage while mourning the loss of her TV family. Her face is powdered white, her lips colorless, and her body stiff, foreshadowing the corpse she will soon become. It is not unexpected when the oppression and militarism she so willingly accepts turn on her and exterminate her in a single apocalyptic blast.

GRANGER

The **foil** of Captain Beatty, Granger too is associated with burning. However, the warming, beneficial campfire around which hovers his coterie of book people, contrasts with the malicious, doom-filled conflagrations that Beatty sets. Granger is the author of *The Fingers in the Glove; the Proper Relationship between the Individual and Society*, a capsule statement of Bradbury's theme. Granger's pragmatic, uplifting words lead Montag from flight to the safety of the forest.

In contrast to Beatty and his Hound, Granger has his own technological wizardry to apply. To defeat the trail-sniffing Hound, he offers the scent of bobcat, which will dissociate Montag from his former odor by applying a safer olfactory identity. Granger represents the balance that has reentered the world and which will alleviate the Dark Age with a new spark of intellectual light. He reveres his grandfather, a sculptor, for the humanistic spark he left behind. With cities lying in charred heaps at his back, Granger, a twenty-fourth century Moses, guides his fellow rescuers of books toward an undisclosed Promised Land.

THE MECHANICAL HOUND

A reincarnation of the vengeful Furies from Greek mythology and the epitome of modern perverted science, the Hound, a slick electronic hitman formed of copper wire and storage batteries and smelling of blue electricity, is an omnipresent menace capable of storing "so many amino acids, so much sulphur, so much butterfat and alkaline" that he can trail the odor index of ten thousand victims inexorably to their doom. From his snout projects a "four-inch hollow steel needle," which can inject enough morphine or procaine to quell a rat, cat, or chicken within three seconds. Sniffing its quarry via "sensitive capillary hairs in the Nylon-brushed nostrils," the Hound growls, then scuttles silently toward its prey on eight rubber-padded feet. Sighting through the "green-blue neon light" of its multifaceted eyes, it is masterminded by a central command for rapid deployment and near-perfect accuracy.

CRITICAL ESSAYS

DYSTOPIAN FICTION AND *FAHRENHEIT 451*

The term "dystopia" is often used as the antonym of "utopia," a perfect world often imagined to exist in the future. A dystopia, therefore, is a terrible place. It might be more helpful (and also more accurate) to conceive of a dystopian literary tradition, a literary tradition which has created worlds that contain reactions against certain ominous social trends and therefore imagines a disastrous future if these trends are not reversed. Most commonly cited as the model of a twentieth-century dystopian novel is Yevgeny Zamiatin's *We* (1924), which envisions an oppressive but stable social order accomplished only through the complete effacement of the individual. *We*, which might more properly be called an anti-utopian work rather than a dystopian work, is often cited as the progenitor of George Orwell's *1984* (1948), a nightmarish vision of a totalitarian world of the future, similar to the one portrayed in *We*, in which order is maintained through terroristic force.

These two novels are often cited as classic dystopian fictions, along with Aldous Huxley's *Brave New World* (1932), which, contrary to popular belief, has a somewhat different purpose and object of attack than the previously mentioned novels. Huxley's *Brave New World* has as its target two distinct works which were representations of a blind faith in the idea of social and technological progress. According to Robert Nisbet, in his *History of the Idea of Progress*, "The idea of progress holds that mankind has advanced in the past—from some aboriginal condition of primitiveness, barbarism, and even nullity—is now advancing, and will continue to advance through the foreseeable future." Two other such works are H. G. Wells' *Men Like Gods* (1923) and, if Brian Stableford is correct (writing in Nicholls, *The Science Fiction Encyclopedia*), J. B. S. Haldane's *Daedalus* (1924). Both of these works are technocratic visions of better times accomplished through technological innovation and exhibit a faith in the idea of progress.

According to Stableford, Bertrand Russell's response to Haldane's *Daedalus*, entitled *Icarus, or the Future of Science* (1924), "linked technology to one of the essential dystopian anxieties: oppression." It became commonplace for dystopian thinkers to believe that regimentation was "a corollary to technological progress." These convictions are present in works such as *Brave New World* and are also present in much of Bradbury's work.

In contrast to dystopian novels like Huxley's and Orwell's, however, Bradbury's *Fahrenheit 451* does not picture villainous dictators (like Orwell's O'Brien) or corrupt philosopher-kings (like Huxley's Mustapha Mond), although Bradbury's Captain Beatty shares a slight similarity to the latter. The crucial difference is that Bradbury's novel does not focus on a ruling elite nor does it portray the society from above, but instead portrays the means of oppression and regimentation through the life of an uneducated and complacent, though ultimately honest and virtuous, working-class hero (Montag). In contrast, Orwell and Huxley choose to portray the lives of petty bureaucrats (Winston Smith and Bernard Marx, respectively), whose alienated lives share similarities to the literary characters of Franz Kafka (1883–1924).

Nonetheless, there are points of similarity between these works. All three imagine a technocratic social order maintained through oppression and regimentation and by the complete efface-ment of the individual (as does Zamiatin). All of these authors envi-sion a populace distracted by the pursuit of vicarious images, which has the effect of creating politically enervated individuals.

Huxley envisions a World State in which war has been eradi-cated in order to achieve social stability; Bradbury and Orwell imag-ine war itself as achieving the same end—by keeping the populace cowering in fear of an enemy attack. The war maintains the status quo because any change in leaders may topple the defense struc-ture. Both Orwell and Bradbury imagine the political usefulness of the anesthetization of experience: all experience becomes form without substance. Both Bradbury and Huxley imagine the use of chemical sedatives and tranquilizers as a means of compensating for the individual's alienated existence. More importantly, all three authors imagine a technocratic social order is accomplished through suppression of books—that is, through *censorship*.

A crucial distinction can be drawn between these books despite their similarities. If the failure of the proles reveals Orwell's despair at the British working-class' political consciousness, and if Mus-tapha Mond reveals Huxley's cynical view of the intellectual, Guy Montag's personal victory over the system represents American optimism. This train of thought leads us back to Henry David Tho-reau, whose *Civil Disobedience* Bradbury must surely hold in high esteem. Recall the remark by Juan Ramón Jiménez that serves as an epigraph to the book: "If they give you ruled paper, write the other way." This could have easily served as Thoreau's motto and is proof of Bradbury's interest in individual freedom. Bradbury's trust in the virtue of the individual and his belief in the inherently corrupt nature of government is a central concept of *Fahrenheit 451*.

THE ISSUE OF CENSORSHIP

The First Amendment to the United States Constitution reads:

> Congress shall make no law respecting an establish-ment of religion, or prohibiting the free exercise thereof; or abridging the freedom of speech or of the press; or the right of the people peaceably to assem-

ble, and to petition the government for redress of grievances.

The common reading of the First Amendment is that commitment to free speech is not the acceptance of non-controversial expressions which enjoy general approval. To accept a commitment to the First Amendment means, in the words of Justice Holmes, "freedom for the thought we hate." As quoted in *Students' Right to Read* (NCTE, 1982), "Censorship leaves students with an inadequate and distorted picture of the ideals, values, and problems of their culture. Writers may often be the spokesmen of their culture, or they may stand to the side, attempting to describe and evaluate that culture. Yet, partly because of censorship or the fear of censorship, many writers are ignored or inadequately represented in the public schools, and many are represented in anthologies not by their best work but by their safest or least offensive work." What are the issues involved in censorship?

Let's imagine that a group is seeking to ban "Goldilocks and the Three Bears" because Goldilocks defies authority. For the sake of argument, let's assume for a moment that you wish to "ban" from the library shelves "Goldilocks and the Three Bears." You must do a number of things. First, you must establish why defying authority is wrong. What are its consequences? What are the probable effects on youth to see flagrant disregard for authority? (In regard to these questions, you might read Plato's *Apology* to get a sense of how to argue the position. It is always a good idea to read and study others who have written on similar issues.) Second, you must have some theory of psychology, either implied or explicitly stated. That is, you must establish how a reading of "Goldilocks and the Three Bears" would inspire a child to flagrant disregard of authority. Why can reading be bad for a child? *How* can it be bad? Next, you must establish how a child who reads "Goldilocks and the Three Bears" will read the book and extract from it a message which says, "Defy Authority Whenever Possible," and then act on this message.

Whatever argument you construct must then be reconciled with responsibilities that go with accepting the rights given by the First Amendment. Perhaps you should consider and think about issues of free speech and fundamental rights which may have not been considered by you before. Indeed, your essay may come down to the simple fact that you cannot claim your own right to *expression* if you feel you have the right to *suppress* the rights of others to express themselves.

REVIEW QUESTIONS AND ESSAY TOPICS

(1) Using specific examples from the novel to support your answer discuss Bradbury's attitude toward literature.

(2) Compare and contrast the philosophical attitudes of Clarisse McClellan and Millie Montag.

(3) In the novel, Montag reads Matthew Arnold's "Dover Beach" to Millie and her friends. Show how the situation described in this poem is an accurate representation of Montag's futuristic society.

(4) Discuss the dual image of fire in the novel.

(5) Trace the steps which lead to Montag's decision to preserve books rather than destroy them.

(6) Examine the psychological complexity of Captain Beatty. Account for his knowledge of books, while also accounting for his desire to burn them.

(7) The image of television recurs throughout the novel. Explain the significance of its recurrence and be sure to detail Montag's attitude towards it.

(8) Write a paper on the literature of dystopian fiction and explain how *Fahrenheit 451* partakes of this tradition.

(9) Explain how the titles to the three parts of the book are significant to the general action that occurs within each part.

(10) Explain how book burning represents a more general trend toward censorship.

(11) Write a paper detailing the ideological issues involved in censorship.

BRADBURY'S PUBLISHED WORKS

For a comprehensive bibliography up to 1975, see William F. Nolan's *The Ray Bradbury Companion* (Detroit, Michigan: Gale Research, 1975).

Novels

Fahrenheit 451. New York: Ballantine, 1953.
Dandelion Wine. New York: Doubleday, 1957.
Something Wicked This Way Comes. New York: Simon and Schuster, 1962.
The Halloween Tree. New York: Doubleday, 1972.
Death is a Lonely Business. New York: Alfred A. Knopf, 1985.
Folon's Folons. New York: Abrams. 1990.

Short Story Collections

Dark Carnival. Sauk City, Wisconsin: Arkham House, 1947.
The Martian Chronicles. New York: Doubleday, 1950.
The Illustrated Man. New York: Doubleday, 1951.
Timeless Stories for Today and Tomorrow (Editor). New York: Bantam, 1952.
The Golden Apples of the Sun. New York: Doubleday, 1953.
The October Country. New York: Ballantine, 1955.
A Medicine for Melancholy. New York: Doubleday, 1959.
R is for Rocket. New York: Doubleday, 1962.
The Machineries of Joy. New York: Bantam, 1965.
The Vintage Bradbury. New York: Vintage, 1965.
S is for Space. New York: Doubleday, 1966.
I Sing the Body Electric. New York: Alfred A. Knopf, 1969.
Long After Midnight. New York: Alfred A. Knopf, 1975.
The Toynbee Convector. New York: Alfred A. Knopf, 1988.

Poetry

When Elephants Last in the Dooryard Bloomed. New York: Knopf. 1973.

Plays

Pillar of Fire and Other Plays. New York: Bantam, 1975.

The Wonderful Ice Cream Suit and Other Plays. New York: Bantam, 1972.
The Ray Bradbury Theater. USA TV Network.

SELECTED BIBLIOGRAPHY

ALDISS, BRIAN W. *Billion Year Spree: The True History of Science Fiction*. New York: Doubleday, 1973.

AMIS, KINGSLEY. *New Maps of Hell*. New York: Harcourt, Brace, 1960.

BRADBURY, RAY. "Day After Tomorrow: Why Science Fiction?" *Nation* (May 2, 1953) Volume 176, No. 18: 364-367. (Note: this article, ironically, precedes an article by William Murray on censorship, titled "Books are Burning.")

BRADBURY, RAY. "Drunk, and in Charge of a Bicycle." Introduction to *The Stories of Ray Bradbury*. New York: Alfred A. Knopf, 1980.

CHAPMAN, ROBERT S. "Science Fiction of the Fifties: Billy Graham, McCarthy and the Bomb," *Foundation* 7-8 (March 1975): 38-52.

DIMEO, STEVEN. "Man and Apollo: A Look at Religion in the Science Fantasies of Ray Bradbury," *Journal of Popular Culture*. 1971.

GREENBERG, MARTIN H. and JOSEPH D. OLANDER, Eds. *Ray Bradbury*. New York: Taplinger, 1980.

HILLEGAS, MARK R. *The Future as Nightmare*. New York: Oxford University Press, 1967.

JOHNSON, WAYNE L. *Ray Bradbury*. New York: Frederick Ungar, 1980.

KIRK, RUSSELL. "The World of Ray Bradbury," *Enemies of Permanent Things*. New Rochelle, NY: Arlington House, 1969.

MOGEN, DAVID. *Ray Bradbury*. Boston: Twayne, 1986.

NICHOLLS, PETER, General Ed. *The Science Fiction Encyclopedia.* Garden City, New York: Doubleday, 1979.

NOLAN, WILLIAM F. *The Ray Bradbury Companion.* Detroit, Michigan: Gale Research, 1975.

NOLAN, WILLIAM F. *3 to the Highest Power.* New York: Avon, 1968.

PRIESTLY, J. B. "Thoughts in the Wilderness: They Come From Inner Space," *New Statesman and Nation* (England). December 5, 1953.

SISARIO, PETER. "A Study of Allusions in Bradbury's *Fahrenheit 451,*" *English Journal.* February, 1970.

SULLIVAN, ANITA T. "Ray Bradbury and Fantasy," *English Journal.* December, 1972.

TOUPONCE, WILLIAM F. *Ray Bradbury and the Poetics of Reverie: Fantasy, Science Fiction, and the Reader.* Ann Arbor, Michigan: UMI Research Press, 1984.

WOLHEIM, DONALD A. *The Universe Makers.* New York: Harper & Row, 1971.

SELECTED BIBLIOGRAPHY ON INTELLECTUAL FREEDOM AND CENSORSHIP

BOLLINGHER, LEE C. *The Tolerant Society, Freedom of Speech and Extremist Speech in America.* Oxford University Press, 1988.

BOSMAJIAN, HAIG A., Ed. *The Freedom to Read.* Neal-Schuman Publishers, 1987.

BURRESS, LEE and EDWARD JENKINSON, Eds. *Students' Right to Know.* National Council of Teachers of English, 1982.

COX, ARCHIBALD. *Freedom of Expression.* Harvard University Press, 1981.

COX, BENJAMIN C. *The Censorship Game and How to Play It*. National Council for the Social Studies, 1977.

DAVIS, JAMES C., Ed. *Dealing with Censorship*. National Council of Teachers of English, 1979.

DONNERSTEIN, EDWARD, DANIEL LINZ, and STEVEN PENROD. *The Question of Pornography: Research Findings and Policy Implications*. Free Press, 1987.

Essentials of English. National Council of Teachers of English, 1982.

FRISHMAN, BOB. *American Families, Responding to the Pro-Family Movement*. People for the American Way, 1984.

GABLER, MEL and NORMAN GABLER (with JAMES C. HEFLEY). *What Are They Teaching Our Children*. SP Publications (Wheaton, IL), 1985.

HENTHOFF, NAT. *The First Freedom*. Delecorte, 1980.

The Hatch Amendment Regulations: A Guidelines Document. American Association of School Administrators, 1985.

INGELHART, LOUIS E. *Press Law and Press Freedom for High School Publications*. Greenwood Press, 1986.

Intellectual Freedom Manual, 2nd Ed. American Library Association Office of Intellectual Freedom, 1983.

JENKINSON, EDWARD. *Censors in the Classroom*. Southern Illinois University Press, 1979.

_____. *The Schoolbook Protest Movement: 40 Questions and Answers*. Phi Delta Kappa Educational Foundation, 1986.

LONDON, HERBERT. *Why Are They Lying to Our Children?* Stein and Day, 1985.

MOFFETT, JAMES. *Storm in the Mountains: A Case Study of Censorship, Conflict and Consciousness*. Southern Illinois University Press, 1988.

MOYER, WAYNE and WILLIAM MAYER. *A Consumer's Guide to Biology Textbooks, 1985.* People for the American Way, 1985.

O'NEIL, ROBERT. *Classrooms in the Crossfire.* Indiana University Press, 1981.

PARKER, BARBARA and STEFANIE WEISS. *Protecting the Freedom to Learn.* People for the American Way, 1983.

PLATO. *The Last Days of Socrates.* Penguin, 1969.

RUBIN, DAVID. *The Rights of Teachers, An ACLU Handbook.* Bantam Books, 1984.

PRICE, JANET, ALAN and CARY LEVIN, Eds. *The Rights of Students, An ACLU Handbook,* 3rd edition. Southern Illinois University Press, 1988.

SOBLE, ALAN. *Pornography: Marxism, Feminism, and the Future of Sexuality.* Yale University Press, 1986.

Students' Right to Read. National Council of Teachers of English, 1982.

TEDFORD, THOMAS L. *Freedom of Speech in the United States.* Random House, 1985.

VITZ, PAUL C. *Censorship: Evidence of Bias in Our Children's Textbooks.* Servant Books, 1986.